# The Hands-On
# RANCH
# BOOK

# The Hands-On RANCH BOOK

HOW TO TIE A KNOT,
START A GARDEN, SADDLE A HORSE,
*and* EVERYTHING ELSE PEOPLE
USED TO KNOW HOW TO DO

## MARY HEFFERNAN

Revell

a division of Baker Publishing Group
Grand Rapids, Michigan

Published by Revell
a division of Baker Publishing Group
Grand Rapids, Michigan
www.revellbooks.com

Printed in the United States of America

Library of Congress Cataloging-in-Publication Data
Names: Heffernan, Mary, 1978– author.
Title: The hands-on ranch book : how to tie a knot, start a garden, saddle a horse, and everything else people used to know how to do / Mary Heffernan.
Description: Grand Rapids, Michigan : Revell, a division of Baker Publishing Group, [2023] | Audience: Ages 9–12 | Audience: Grades 4–6
Identifiers: LCCN 2023001295 | ISBN 9780800742911 (paperback) | ISBN 9780800745110 (casebound) | ISBN 9781493443550 (ebook)
Subjects: LCSH: Handicraft—Juvenile literature. | Life skills—Juvenile literature. | Sustainable living—Juvenile literature.
Classification: LCC TT157 .H383 2023 | DDC 680—dc23/eng/20230213
LC record available at https://lccn.loc.gov/2023001295

The author is represented by the literary agency of Stoker Literary, Inc.

Interior design by William Overbeeke

Baker Publishing Group publications use paper produced from sustainable forestry practices and post-consumer waste whenever possible.

23  24  25  26  27  28  29       7  6  5  4  3  2  1

*To my four little Marys . . .*

always on an adventure to learn.

# Contents

Introduction   8

## Part 1
### • COUNTRY LIVING •

How to Predict the Weather . . . . . . . . . . . . . . . 12

How to Read a Map . . . . . . . . . . . . . . . . . . 14

How to Use a Compass . . . . . . . . . . . . . . . . 16

How to Find Water . . . . . . . . . . . . . . . . . . 19

How to Purify Water . . . . . . . . . . . . . . . . . 20

How to Build a Fire . . . . . . . . . . . . . . . . . . 22

How to Build a Simple Shelter . . . . . . . . . . . . 25

How to Identify Animal Tracks . . . . . . . . . . . . 26

How to Make a Fishing Pole and Hook . . . . . . . 28

Understanding the Water Cycle . . . . . . . . . . . 30

Working with Tools . . . . . . . . . . . . . . . . . . 32

How to Start a Garden . . . . . . . . . . . . . . . . 36

A Day in the Life of a Rancher . . . . . . . . . . . . 44

## Part 2
### • DO IT YOURSELF •

How to Make a Wild Earth Dye . . . . . . . . . . . 48

How to Dye, Card, and Spin Wool . . . . . . . . . . 51

Breadmaking and Baking . . . . . . . . . . . . . . . . . . . . 54

Cooking and Grilling Basics . . . . . . . . . . . . . . . . . 62

Candlemaking . . . . . . . . . . . . . . . . . . . . . . . . . . . . 72

Leatherwork . . . . . . . . . . . . . . . . . . . . . . . . . . . . . 74

How to Make Maple Syrup . . . . . . . . . . . . . . . . . . 76

Simple Sewing Fixes . . . . . . . . . . . . . . . . . . . . . . . 80

Create an Irrigation System . . . . . . . . . . . . . . . . . 84

Four Important Knots to Know . . . . . . . . . . . . . . . 86

## Part 3
### • ANIMALS •

Horses . . . . . . . . . . . . . . . . . . . . . . . . . . . . . . . . . . 93

Chickens . . . . . . . . . . . . . . . . . . . . . . . . . . . . . . . 103

Cattle . . . . . . . . . . . . . . . . . . . . . . . . . . . . . . . . . . 111

Sheep . . . . . . . . . . . . . . . . . . . . . . . . . . . . . . . . . 121

Rabbits . . . . . . . . . . . . . . . . . . . . . . . . . . . . . . . . 131

Working Dogs . . . . . . . . . . . . . . . . . . . . . . . . . . . 137

## Part 4
### • FOR YOUNG ENTREPRENEURS •

Putting Your Talents to Work! . . . . . . . . . . . . . . . 146

Raising Animals for Profit . . . . . . . . . . . . . . . . . . 150

Interesting Careers . . . . . . . . . . . . . . . . . . . . . . . 152

*Acknowledgments   158*

# Introduction

**W**e are all more capable than we think we are. Whether it's growing our own food, navigating with a compass, building a fire, or caring for animals— there really isn't a more satisfying feeling than being capable and knowledgeable in a situation where we need to think on our feet, make decisions, and solve problems.

Living on a ranch means we have lots of opportunities to learn new skills and find ways to solve problems as they arise. We have to be thinkers and doers, and a lot is expected of every member of the family. Raising livestock is a full-time job, and there are no days off.

As a family, it's our responsibility to care for our animals in the sunshine and rain, at sunrise and after dark, when they are healthy and when one falls ill. No matter how much we plan for, there are always new challenges that arise on a daily basis that we have to solve together or on our own.

It's a big responsibility and a lot of work, but when we come in after a long day to eat a late dinner (we don't eat until the animals are fed!) and sit together by the fire, we all feel so satisfied and get to share about our day—funny stories, challenges, and things we are proud that we accomplished.

When we moved to the ranch, my four girls ranged in age from six years old down to one year old—and they had to learn all of these skills out of necessity. We had a lot to do and a lot to take care of. They became independent thinkers and capable ranch hands. They learned to climb a fence, saddle a horse, and use a saw to cut firewood. They learned to bottle-feed a calf and warm a baby lamb by the fire. They learned to care for a home and cook dinner when they needed to.

We've all learned so many skills on the ranch, and we are eager to help you learn some of them too—building a campfire, caring for an animal, bottle-feeding a lamb, starting a garden, mending a jacket, saddling a horse, cooking food we've grown and raised ourselves, and so much more.

You don't have to grow up on a ranch to learn new things about animals and the outdoors. We hope you enjoy these skills and lessons we've learned along the way that we get to share with you!

Happy trails!

Mary

Francie    Maisie

JJ    Tessa

Part 1

# COUNTRY LIVING

# How to Predict the Weather

**D**id you know that all of the weather and seasons on Earth are created by the sun? As Earth rotates round and round, the sun will heat different areas of our planet's surface. This causes changes to the atmosphere. As moisture is added through evaporation, clouds form, winds pick up, and more.

The earth's axis is tilted, and while the earth rotates, it is also making a big loop around the sun. One year—365 days—is equal to one trip around the sun. During that year, we experience all of the seasons: summer, autumn, winter, and spring. The tilt of the earth's axis causes areas to receive more or less sunlight at certain points during the year. This changes the temperature and weather patterns, creating different seasons.

Today, weather predictions are made using modern technology and can be viewed on the news, internet, and weather apps. But there are still ways to predict the weather without technology, such as observing cloud size and shape. There are many different types of clouds, but here are a few of the most common ones!

**Cirrus** clouds look very wispy and scattered throughout the sky. They may appear in fair weather.

**Cirrocumulus** clouds are made up of smaller clouds called cloudlets. They are pretty evenly spaced throughout the sky. These clouds usually appear in fair weather but also mean that storms could be coming in the near future.

**Cirrostratus** clouds are widespread through the sky and sometimes give off a halo effect. These clouds typically appear before a warm front and rain.

**Cumulus** clouds are puffy in shape—think of a cauliflower head! You can usually see these clouds on bright sunny days, but they may turn into **cumulonimbus clouds** that are likely to produce rain and thunderstorms.

**Stratus** clouds are low, thick clouds that blanket the sky. Stratus clouds may bring light drizzle or snow.

You can also tell if the weather will change by watching the way clouds move. If the clouds are all moving in the same direction, or if they don't seem to be moving at all, the weather will likely stay the same. If the clouds are moving in two directions, the weather will likely change in the next few hours.

# How to Read a Map

**K**nowing how to read a map is a skill that is less common than it used to be . . . but what a fabulous skill to have! If you ever find yourself without a cell phone or in a place that does not get cell signal (no GPS!), being able to pick up a map and navigate yourself to where you want to go could really come in handy.

There are several different types of maps, but here are some details you'll find on all of them.

**Title.** Each map contains a title to let you know which kind of map it is. *Topographic maps* are great for hikers, as they depict important information such as terrain, elevation, and distances. *Road maps* contain information that is necessary for someone driving, like interstates and city names. *Tourist maps* are great for someone visiting a new place and looking for landmarks, hotels, museums, and so forth.

**Legend.** Since there are so many different types of maps, cartographers (mapmakers) include a legend to explain what the different shapes and colors mean on that specific map (for example, highways, mountains, borders).

**Orientation.** Most maps are made with north being at the top, but some still include a compass rose to show which way all four cardinal directions are depicted on the map.

**Scale.** Your map will certainly not be drawn full-scale, so it will include a scale of miles to let you know what measurements represent actual distance and size. For example, 1 inch on your map may represent 50 actual miles.

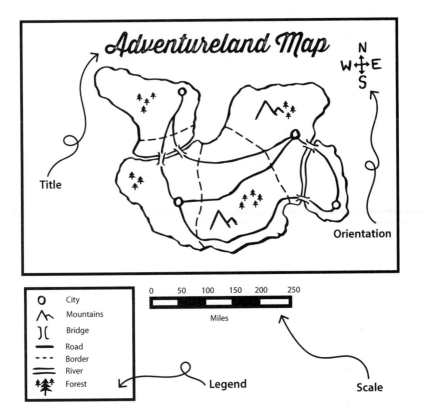

# How to Use a Compass

If you are adventuring in the woods, it's a great idea to carry a compass with you! It's easy to get turned around when many of your surroundings start to blend together and look the same and you don't know which way is north. A compass is a basic navigational tool that works without any batteries and can be used with or without a map. If you've never used a compass before, it can be a bit intimidating, so take time to study your compass and its many parts before you head out on your trip.

The magnetic needle in your compass will point to *magnetic north*, which differs from *true north* by a few degrees. A few degrees may not sound like very much, and sometimes it isn't. Other times it can lead you away from your desired path by several feet—or even miles!

This difference in magnetic north and true north on your compass is known as **declination**. You'll need to adjust your compass for declination before orienting it with the map you're using.

Place your compass on the map so that your **direction of travel arrow** is pointing toward the top of the map. Next, rotate the **bezel** so that north is lined up with the arrow. Keeping your direction of travel arrow pointing north, adjust the **baseplate** of your compass so it is lined up with the edge of your map.

Keeping your compass parallel to your body (about chest high), rotate yourself until the **magnetic needle** in your compass is lined up with the **orienting arrow**.

Find a landmark in the sight line where your needle is pointing on the map—this will help you identify where you are when you're out in the wild. Bring along your compass and your map in case you need to reorient yourself while exploring.

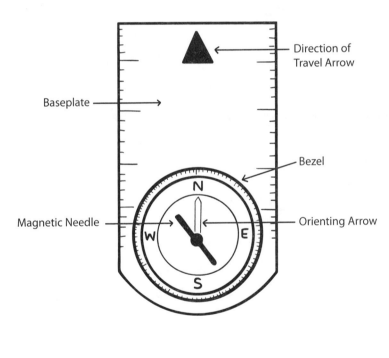

Direction of Travel Arrow

Baseplate

Bezel

Magnetic Needle

Orienting Arrow

# How to Find Water

**W**ater is a necessity for life. Our bodies need it to stay hydrated, produce saliva, digest food, and many more things. Without water, we are not able to move and perform as well physically. These things are especially important to keep in mind when you are out on long hiking trips and trying to navigate rough terrain.

If you are out in the wilderness and need to find a safe source of drinking water, look for signs and clues of where a freshwater source could be located. Remember that water will flow downhill, so check in places where two hills come together. A small stream will be more likely to flow between them. In addition, pay attention to the vegetation. More fresh green plants will be growing near water. The denser the plant growth, the closer you may be to a water source.

After locating a source of water, make sure to check that the water is decently clean. Draw from locations where the water is flowing or moving. Standing or stagnant water promotes the growth of bacteria that could make you sick. If you are still unsure, sit and watch the wildlife for a while. They will show you where it's safe to drink from.

# How to Purify Water

Once you have collected your water, it is important to clean it no matter how safe you think it is. There are many ways to purify water. Here are just a few to get you started.

### ◆ Filtration Systems ◆

Today there are many manufactured filters you can purchase and bring along with you. This is one of the simplest ways to purify water. Most of these filters work by filling them with water and then allowing it to drip through the system. Others have a straw connected that draws the water through the filter as you suck on it to drink. Check the available models to decide which one is best for you and the type of adventures you plan to use it for.

### ◆ Boiling ◆

This is an age-old method that is simple and straightforward. First, build a fire and get it going. Next, fill a fire-safe container with water, place it over the flames, and allow the water to reach a rapid boil. You will know you have reached boiling when bubbles appear. Let it boil for one minute (if you're at elevations above 6,500 feet, boil for about three minutes) to make sure you kill any potential bacteria or viruses. In the winter, this same method can be used to transform snow into drinking water. As the snow melts, any unwanted microorganisms are also killed by the heat.

## ✦ Collecting Rainwater ✦

Another great method is to simply collect rainwater as it falls from the sky. This can be as simple as setting out multiple containers, although you may not collect much. You can catch even more by stringing up a tarp and funneling everything into a collection barrel.

# How to Build a Fire

**R**emember, fires are hot and can be dangerous, so be sure to have an adult nearby at all times. Keep any younger siblings or pets from getting too close to the flames.

Before starting to build the fire, take some time to collect good supplies. You will need the following materials to build a solid campfire:

- **Tinder**—small, dry pieces of brush and leaves that will easily catch on fire.
- **Kindling**—small to medium twigs and sticks that will catch fire and continue to burn after the tinder is gone.
- **Firewood**—thicker branches and logs. This is the main component of the fire.
- **Extinguisher**—keep a bucket of water or a shovel close by in case of an emergency.

To get the fire started, place your tinder in the center of your ring and use a match, lighter, or flint and pocketknife to produce a flame. Allow the tinder to burn and catch on fire. Gently blowing on it to add oxygen can help the flame to strengthen and grow. Once the tinder has been going for a while, add some kindling on top. Continue to slowly feed the flame small twigs and sticks to maintain consistent growth.

Finally, place the firewood on top. There are many different firewood formations you could look up, including the teepee and the log cabin. Choose one that works for you, and remember . . . it doesn't have to be perfect!

Remember: dry, dead materials that have fallen from trees often make the best campfire materials because they burn so easily.

## ◆ Tending the Fire ◆

Continue to slowly feed the campfire with new firewood. This will ensure the fire does not extinguish, causing you to start all over again. Simply maintaining your fire at a manageable size is the goal.

## ◆ Extinguishing ◆

It's best for campfires to burn all the way down to ash, but if that isn't possible, the best way to extinguish a fire is by dumping water on top. You need to drown ALL of the embers until they stop making a hissing sound.

If you don't have water, shovel dirt or sand on top. This will suffocate the fire and eventually extinguish it. Scrape off any embers from the wood and cover them up with dirt. Continue to add water, dirt, and sand to your campfire until it is cool. Remember, if it's too hot to touch, don't leave it. At that point it is still possible for it to reignite.

# Fire Safety

Fire can be essential for survival. It provides a source of light and heat. Campfires can be useful for cooking, purifying water, and so much more, but a fire can easily become a hazard if not properly handled. It's important to follow these simple steps to build a fire successfully and safely.

Before beginning, make sure you are up to date on any fire restrictions in your area. These rules and regulations are constantly changing. Many places require you to have a burn permit. Check with the US Forest Service, local fire departments, or your campground for the most up-to-date information.

If you are camping at a specified campsite, there is more than likely a fire ring. If so, be sure to use this designated spot to build your fire. In these situations, you should set up your tent at least 15 feet away so that it doesn't catch on fire.

If there is no fire ring available, you will need to dig a fire pit. When deciding on where to dig, look for a place that is flat, open, and far away from any vegetation or brush that could easily catch on fire. Remove any debris such as leaves, sticks, or branches within a 10-foot circle around the campfire's location. In addition, be sure to check on the direction of the wind. Find a place that is blocked from strong gusts. Once your space is clear, you are ready to start digging.

Create a hole in the ground that is at least 12 inches deep. Once the hole has been dug, place rocks around the edge as an additional barrier.

# How to Build a Simple Shelter

**P**art of being an outdoor adventurer is being able to think creatively and work with the resources available to you in nature. And part of building a shelter is experimenting with different designs!

When building a shelter in the woods, think "high and dry" to avoid water. Don't build at the bottom of a hill where water tends to run and pool when it rains. Search for an old log or fallen tree that is leaning over with space between it and the ground. Collect some sturdy, straight branches to lean against the log or tree that you have selected. You'll want to put some insulation in your shelter to keep warm and have something soft to lay on. Moss and pine needles are a great choice for this!

If you have the resources, use rope to tie a tarp over the top of your shelter. Secure the corners so it doesn't fall off or fly away. This will be a game changer to protect yourself from wind and rain!

# How to Identify Animal Tracks

**W**e can learn quite a bit from a simple animal track—things like species and size, how long ago

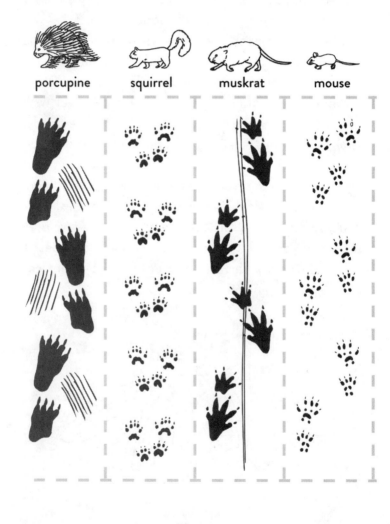

porcupine   squirrel   muskrat   mouse

the animal left the track, and perhaps even what it was doing there.

Sometimes it's very important to know these things, like if you're hunting or adventuring in the outdoors and need to be aware of what wildlife is nearby. Other times it can just be a fun skill to explore!

These two pages show a few tracks you might come across that would be handy to know.

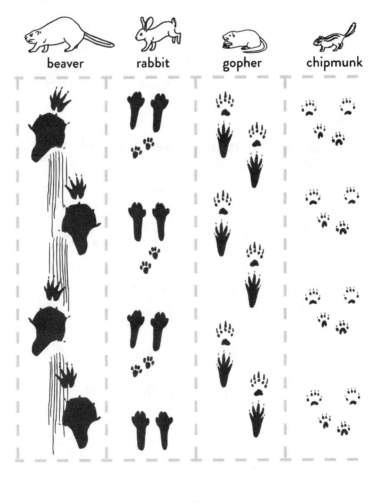

beaver          rabbit          gopher          chipmunk

# How to Make a Fishing Pole and Hook

**F**ishing is an ancient activity that has provided people of all ages with food, sport, and enjoyment for thousands of years. A fishing pole, or rod, is a necessary piece of equipment while fishing. You could go to your local sporting goods store to buy a rod, but when you're out in the woods you can make one with the materials around you.

You want your rod to be about four feet long and have flex. The best material to use for this would be a willow branch that is pretty straight. When you've found your perfect branch, you'll need to attach a line. This is the hardest part because it needs to be very thin but also very strong. Fish have great eyesight, and you don't want them to see the string.

If you are at a mountain lake or stream, there is probably a campsite nearby. People love to bring their horses into these campsites for the night. If you look where you think the horses bedded down, you might find a hair from the tail of a horse. Horsehair is long and thin and will make the perfect fishing line. Tie the horsehair to the end of the willow branch and your rod will be complete!

The last thing needed to catch a fish is a hook. If you have drinks with you, twist off one of the tabs from a soda can. Use a sharp pocketknife to cut the tab at an angle so one side has a sharp edge—and there you'll have your makeshift hook! Dig around for a small bug or worm that you can put on the hook and use as bait.

Now get out there and catch a fish!

# Understanding
# the Water Cycle

Did you know that we cannot create water? What is already here is what we have to use. But another incredible thing about water is that it is part of a large cycle that allows us to use it over and over again. This cycle is called the *water cycle*, and it has three main processes:

**Evaporation.** This is the process of water being removed from the earth's surface. Heat from the sun helps water evaporate and return into the atmosphere as water vapor.

**Condensation.** As water vapor in the atmosphere cools, it condenses to form clouds. Clouds collect water droplets, becoming more and more dense. You have probably experienced condensation on a hot summer day when droplets form on the outside of an ice-cold glass of water.

**Precipitation.** Once the clouds become too dense and heavy, they release droplets of water. Precipitation comes in many forms, such as rain, hail, and snow. As precipitation lands on the ground, it will either soak into the soil or run off into streams, rivers, and lakes. This starts the whole process over again.

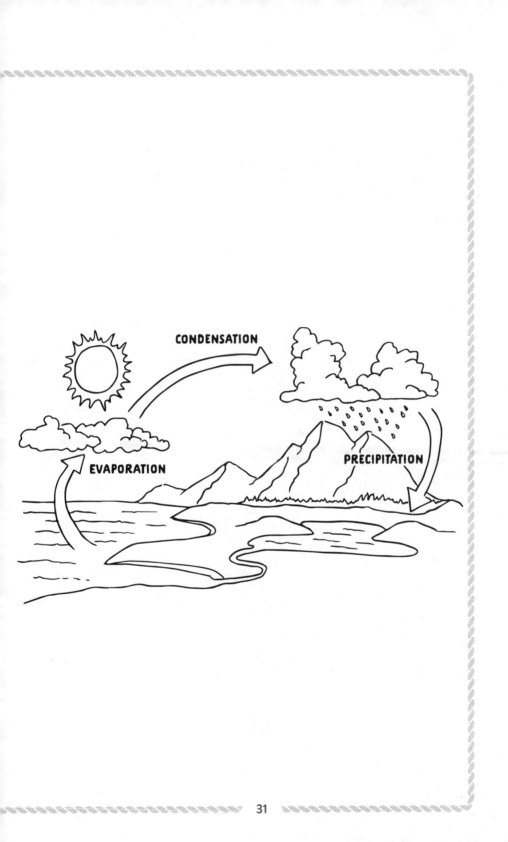

CONDENSATION

EVAPORATION

PRECIPITATION

# Working with Tools

**T**he following hand tools are useful in a variety of projects and are helpful for any household:

- Pliers
- Tape measure
- Sharp craft knife, such as an X-Acto
- Carpenter's square
- Hardpoint timber saw
- Crowbar or wrecking bar
- 16-ounce claw hammer
- Lump hammer
- LOTS of pencils
- Variety of screwdrivers including slotted (or flathead), Phillips, Pozidriv, and Torx. *Having a variety of screwdrivers is a necessity.*
- Set of chisels for both wood and masonry
- Toolbox or sturdy storage system

## ❖ Taking Care of Your Tools ❖

Maintaining your tools is just as important as purchasing quality tools to begin with. Tool upkeep is a fairly easy chore. Start by simply keeping your tools clean and dry. If they get wet, dry them off before putting them away. If there are ever signs of rust, remove it with sandpaper or steel wool. Just be sure to rub a little WD-40 over the location afterward.

Tools with blades, such as saws, should be kept sharp. You are more likely to get hurt and your tool is more likely to break if the blade is dull. Ask an adult to help with blade and power tool repairs. Replace any broken blades as soon as possible.

Other tools may also have breakable parts. Be sure to repair and replace these parts quickly to prevent further breaks or potential injury. When making repairs, do your research, talk to experts near you, or hire someone more knowledgeable to do it instead. A badly repaired tool could be just as dangerous as a broken tool.

After working in dusty or dirty conditions, most tools will benefit from a quick wipe down. This is especially important for power tools. Use compressed air to remove any dust that may have gotten stuck within these tools. Removing debris will help your tools work more smoothly and last longer.

## • Safety First! •

Whenever working with machinery, equipment, and sharp objects, safety should be the number one priority! When people are careless or believe that they won't get hurt, that is when accidents tend to happen. Be sure to follow any safety specifics given to you by equipment manufacturers, teachers, or adults and supervisors. In addition, follow these safety tips to avoid any serious injuries.

- **Wear proper safety gear.** Different tools may require specific safety gear. As a general rule, do not wear loose-fitting clothes, especially when working with mechanical equipment. It is also a good idea to wear sturdy, protective shoes or boots. In situations where there is flying debris or sparks, wear safety glasses or goggles. Use gloves to protect your hands from rough materials and splinters. A hard hat should be worn in locations where there is a risk of falling objects. Other safety gear could include reflective vests, face masks, and ear protection.

- **Take your time.** Rushing through a project and trying to get everything done as quickly as possible will lead to carelessness. A lack of care will likely result in slipups, mistakes, and accidents. Whether they lead to injury or a poorly built project, neither is helpful or ideal.

- **Think it through.** This goes along with taking your time. Before you start a project, take a step back and really think about it. Ask yourself how the plan will be executed. Look for potential risks and figure out how to safely navigate or avoid them. A poorly thought through plan could put your health and safety at risk.

- **Use the right tools and materials.** Using the wrong tools and materials are two of the biggest mistakes you can make. Each tool is specifically designed to complete a certain job. Improvising with the improper tool is not a good idea.

- **Keep a first aid kit.** Purchase a first aid kit or put together your own with a few basics to keep yourself and others safe. A basic first aid kit should include Band-Aids, antiseptic wipes, adhesive tape, tweezers, sterile water, and a variety of gauze rolls and pads. There may be other things that you include that are essential to you, but this is a basic list to get you started.

# How to Start a Garden

**S**tarting a garden is exciting! It is fun to think about all of the yummy produce and beautiful flowers that will be coming your way. Before getting to that point, a lot of thought and planning must go into a garden. Two things to think about before you begin planting are the location and size of your garden.

When it comes to location, the most important thing is to look for a sunny spot away from any trees or large shrubs that would produce a lot of shade. Avoid low ground where rain collects so that your plants do not receive too much water. If possible, find a location close to a water source to make irrigation easier. Keep in mind that very few people have an "ideal" location. Just choose the best spot you can.

Here are a few factors you should consider when determining how large your garden should be:

- **Purpose.** Why are you planting a garden? If you are trying to feed your family, think about how many people will be eating food. Gardeners looking to can or preserve their harvest will need to produce a lot more. If you are just doing it for fun, a smaller garden may be a better place to start.
- **Vegetable selection.** Think about the crops you intend to plant. Some vegetables can require up to three feet of space in order to grow well.

- **Available space.** Depending on where you live, you might have room for a larger garden. But maybe you can only plant in garden boxes or pots. That's still gardening!
- **Time.** The larger the garden, the more time will be required to maintain the space. Think about how much time you have to devote to your garden.

There are a couple of ways to get a garden started. You can go and buy plant starts from a nursery or greenhouse. These are plants that have sprouted from seeds and have already grown a decent root system. You can bring them home and transplant them into the ground or into pots of your choosing.

Another option is to plant seeds yourself. This is called *sowing* seeds. Follow these simple steps to start plants from seeds!

1. Gather containers or trays that could be used to grow seeds in. Seed starter kits are great for getting seeds going, but egg cartons and small containers work too. Fill them with soil.

2. Using your finger or a pen, create a small hole (about ¼ inch deep) in each container.

3. Open the seed packet and place a couple seeds in each container. Be sure to read the directions on the packet for specific instructions.

4. Cover the seeds by pushing soil over the top and then add some water.

5. Set the containers in a sunny location away from any hazards. Monitor daily and water as needed.

Once your seeds have had time to sprout, grow, and establish a decent root system, it is time to plant them outdoors. Wait until the weather is warm enough and all chance of frost is past. Be gentle when removing plants from their containers and transplanting them to the garden.

### ◆ How to Read a Seed Packet ◆

When starting a garden, you will probably need to buy some packets of seeds. Seed packets contain loads of information, including instructions for planting, guides for spacing, and projected time until maturity. Some packets may look different from the one shown here and may contain more information than this one does, but this sample packet shows the most important information and instructions. Let's check it out!

The **seed depth** tells us how deep to plant the seed for proper germination.

The **plant space** tells us how much room to leave between tomato plants. When planting seeds, we have to consider the size of the mature plant.

**"Sprouts in"** refers to the number of days it takes a seed to germinate and for the first green leaves to poke through the soil.

**"Matures in"** refers to the number of days it takes for a plant to grow large and produce fruit—in this example, how long it will take the plant to produce tomatoes. Sometimes this will be labeled as "Days Until Harvest."

The **planting** or "How to Grow" section is the most important. Here, you will find the specifics about how to sow these seeds, whether they need to be in direct sunlight or shade, and what sort of climate they need for proper growth.

The **seed count** refers to the number of seeds in the packet.

The **germination rate** tells us what percentage of the seeds will actually germinate and produce plants.

Somewhere on every seed packet you will find a date and a location of production. Fresh seeds have the best germination rate, but you can plant seeds from previous years as well.

# HEIRLOOM TOMATO

| SEED DEPTH | PLANT SPACE | SPROUTS IN | MATURES IN |
| --- | --- | --- | --- |
| 1/4" | 12–24" | 7–15 DAYS | 80 DAYS |

## PLANTING

Start seeds indoors 6-8 weeks before the last spring frost, and transplant in late spring after nights have warmed. Sow outdoors in climates with 120 or more frost-free days. Plant in direct sunlight. Allow tomatoes to ripen on the vine before harvesting.

| SEED COUNT | GERMINATION RATE |
| --- | --- |
| 80 | 90% |

PACKED FOR 2021 • GROWN IN THE USA

## • How to Read a Hardiness Zone Chart •

To make sure your garden has plants that grow well in your location, you can use the Plant Hardiness Zone Map from the US Department of Agriculture. It shows eleven zones in the US that are determined by average minimum temperature (that is, the coldest it usually gets). This map is updated every few years, and you can find the most recent version at https://PlantHardiness.ARS.USDA.gov.

To see which zone you are in, find your state on the map and zoom in on your town's general location. Match the color from the map to the corresponding color on the map legend, and that is your plant hardiness zone.

# ◆ Tools for Gardening and Growing ◆

Gardens can be wet and muddy! A pair of rain or muck **boots** will keep your feet warm and dry.

A **shovel** is used for digging and lifting soil, compost, and other bulky materials.

**Aerators** help loosen the soil so air, water, and other nutrients can get in.

A **trowel** is a small handheld shovel that is useful for planting seeds and plant starts.

A **watering can** is the easiest tool to use to make sure your plants have water. Even in winter, don't forget to water your plants!

**Pruning shears** are sharp and are used to trim or remove part of a plant.

The "teeth" of a **rake** help gather up and spread loose items such as leaves, grass, or hay.

**Wheelbarrows** are hand-powered carts used for carrying heavy loads. They are easy enough to navigate on uneven ground and in tight spaces.

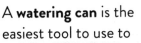

## ◆ When to Harvest Your Garden ◆

When deciding if it is time to harvest your garden, look for different characteristics based on the type of fruit and where it is produced. Orchardists and farmers depend on their knowledge and senses to give them clues about whether fruits are ripe. These clues are found in smell, shape, color, taste, and firmness.

Depending on the type of fruit, harvesting may occur before it has reached full ripeness, such as bananas and pears. These fruits will continue to ripen once they are picked. That is why you will often find green bananas in the grocery store that will eventually turn yellow on your kitchen counter. Figs, blueberries, and some other fruits must be either preserved or consumed within a few days of being harvested because they completely ripen on the branch. Other fruits can be "stored" on the branch before being picked.

- **Oranges**—To tell if your orange is ready to harvest, feel for a thin, smooth skin that doesn't have any soft spots. You should also be able to smell a sweet, fragrant aroma.
- **Apples**—When apples are ripe, they will naturally start to drop from the trees. Apple trees do this to self-seed and reproduce. When picking apples, cup one in your hand while giving it a slight twist . . . it should come off easily! You can tell if apples are getting rotten when they look and feel soft or mushy. If they aren't ripe yet, they will be quite hard and taste sour.

- **Lemons**—Ripe lemons can be detected by their size, not just their color. When your lemons have grown to about two inches in diameter and their skin looks glossy, they are ripe and ready to be harvested. Lemons prefer to ripen on the tree . . . so be careful not to pick them too early!
- **Garlic** is ready to be harvested about 90 to 110 days after it is planted. If you lose track of time, dig up some of the garlic and if it looks like the cloves are filling out the skin, they are ready to be harvested!
- **Potatoes** can be harvested as early as 45 to 55 days after planting. When you see blossoms appear on the plants, that's a sign that they are ready to harvest (or will be very soon). It's a great time digging around in the dirt for your potatoes!
- **Pumpkins** are ready to harvest about four months after sowing. You'll notice the leaves start to die and the fruit will become a rich orange. Your pumpkins should be hard to the touch and shouldn't dent easily.

# A Day in the Life of a Rancher

Every day the Heffernan girls have many chores to do and responsibilities to fulfill at Five Marys Farms. There are animals to be fed, rooms to be cleaned, and homework to get done. Even though it is a lot of work, the girls know that chores are a necessary part of life.

On a typical school day, the girls will wake up by 7 a.m., get ready for their day, make their beds, and feed any bottle babies they might have at the time. JJ and Tessa will also feed the horses and their 4-H steers in the morning. Then they all go to school.

In the evening, bottle babies need to be fed again, and the girls make sure to get their homework done before any fun activities. It is also Maisie and Francie's turn to split the responsibility of feeding the horses and 4-H steers.

In addition to daily chores, the girls help out in many other ways. A few times a week they will help with a quick cleanup in the living room or kitchen. There are always dishes to be washed, blankets to pick up, and counters to be wiped down.

Occasionally, they are also asked to help out with jobs as they come up around the ranch, such as fixing a fence or sorting cattle.

# A Rancher's Typical Day

4:30 A.M.  Alarm

4:45 A.M.  Coffee

5:00 A.M.  Feeding livestock off the feed truck

6:30 A.M.  Working cattle

7:30 A.M.  Meet the brand inspector

7:45 A.M.  Walk steers up to the barn for harvest

8:15 A.M.  Fix something . . . because there's always something broken!

9:00 A.M.  Harvest team starts for the day

11:00 A.M.  Check in with the farm store where orders are shipping out

11:30 A.M.  Lunch break at Five Marys Burgerhouse

12:30 P.M.  Back to the ranch to work sheep

3:00 P.M.  Load the feed truck for afternoon feeding

4:45 P.M.  Sort cattle for the next day's harvest

5:30 P.M.  Fix the generator—again

6:30 P.M.  Bring more firewood down to the house

7:00 P.M.  Family dinner and prayers

8:00 P.M.  Enjoy the end of the night by the fire

Part 2

# DO IT YOURSELF

# How to Make
# a Wild Earth Dye

**W**ild earth dyes are colorful pigments that are found in nature. They are most often sourced from the roots, stems, flowers, and leaves of plants. They may also be sourced from tree bark, fruits and nuts, insects, shells, and minerals.

Since water is typically neutral or sometimes alkaline and makes up the largest part of most dye solutions, the solutions tend to be neutral or alkaline. Any acid is usually washed out or greatly reduced due to the amount of water. The addition of vinegar (or another highly acidic substance) reintroduces acid into the dye solution, which creates more binding opportunities between the pigment and the fabric or egg being dyed. This can sometimes result in a more vibrant or permanent color.

Natural materials were the original sources of dyes and paints. They were used to create beautiful paintings and colorful textiles. Synthetic dyes are commonly used today, but some people still prefer the creativity and eco-friendly nature of nonsynthetic materials.

Using food in dyes is an absolutely wonderful way to create some beautiful colored fabrics. You'll have a blast experimenting with different items and seeing what colors they provide. Some may surprise you!

The key to creating rich colors is to leave your fabric or eggs in the dye substance overnight. To add some creative elements, tie your fabric in knots or loop rubber bands around it!

Here's a list of ideas to start with . . .

- Red beets
- Turmeric powder
- Blueberries
- Carrots
- Cayenne powder
- Orange peels
- Coffee
- Tea
- Black beans

- Spinach
- Raspberries
- Pomegranate juice
- Activated charcoal
- Onion skins
- Red cabbage
- Paprika
- Cherries
- Blackberries

The following dye recipes will make enough to color eggs in a bowl. Adjust your measurements to larger quantities if you'll be dyeing fabrics.

**?!**
*Ask an Adult*

**Turmeric** (creates yellow or gold dye): Stir 2 tablespoons turmeric powder into 1 cup boiling water. Add 2 teaspoons white vinegar. Add eggs and soak overnight.

**Yellow and purple onions** (creates brown, orange, or red dye): Take the skins from 6 onions and simmer in 2 cups of water for 15 minutes. Strain out the skins and allow liquid to cool. Add 3 teaspoons of white vinegar. Add eggs and soak overnight. For a marbling effect, wrap your eggs in onion skins.

**Activated charcoal** (creates black or gray dye): Boil 3 cups of water. Add ⅓ cup charcoal and dissolve.

Add 2 tablespoons white vinegar. Add eggs and soak for 8 to 24 hours.

**Red cabbage** (creates deep blue or purple dye): Cut ¼ head of red cabbage into chunks and add to 4 cups boiling water. Stir in 2 tablespoons of white vinegar. Add eggs and soak for a few hours or overnight. The longer you keep the eggs in the dye, the deeper color you will achieve.

# How to Dye, Card, and Spin Wool

**W**ool is a fiber produced by sheep, alpacas, and other mammals. When an animal is sheared, the fleece fibers can be split into two groups: guard hair and the wool undercoat. The wool undercoat is what is used to produce warm textiles such as yarn and fleece. The fibers are small, soft, and crimped. Wool is what provides animals with warmth.

The skin of most wool-producing animals secretes an oily wax called *lanolin*. It's all over the wool fibers, so when you work with these animals or handle their wool, it will end up on your hands and actually make your hands very soft and hydrated. In fact, some people harvest lanolin and make it into lotions and soaps to rejuvenate the skin.

It is a long process to take the wool from an animal and transform it into a textile. The many steps include shearing, skirting, cleaning, scouring, grading, sorting, carding, dyeing, spinning, weaving, and finishing. Traditionally, everything used to be done by hand, taking spinners at least twenty hours to produce one skein of yarn! Machines make this process a lot faster now, but some people still take the time to do it manually. Here are a few steps you can learn to do at home.

**Carding** refers to the step that removes any leftover dirt or plant matter from the fibers. The wool is moved through a series of teeth or brushes that straighten and streamline the individual fibers.

**Dyeing** is the process of adding color to your yarn. Wool can absorb about 30 percent of its weight in water. This allows each fiber to absorb the dye well.

Both natural and synthetic dyes can be used for coloring wool fibers. Using tea is a great way to dye wool that produces a gorgeous array of natural colors. Here are some easy steps for how to do that:

1. Create a tea mixture in a large pot. Gather teabags and steep them in a large pot of hot water. You'll need to play around with how many tea bags you use depending on the richness of color that you like. Add 1 teaspoon of white vinegar to every 1 cup of water that you use. After you have reached your desired color, let the mixture cool to room temperature.

2. While your tea mixture is reaching room temperature, pre-soak your yarn in a solution of 1 part white vinegar to 4 parts lukewarm water—enough to cover your yarn. Let the yarn soak for about 30 minutes, then squeeze out any excess liquid.

3. Add your wool to the tea mixture and soak overnight.

4. Remove wool from the tea mixture and rinse in a large bucket filled with lukewarm water. Squeeze out excess liquid and hang to dry.

**Spinning** is a process where weaker fibers are combined with stronger fibers to form yarn. The spinning machine twists and moves to combine the fibers, which have crimping and rough surfaces that cause them to stick together.

If you want to spin wool by hand, attach a **spindle hook** to the wool. Let the spindle hang from the wool and begin to spin the spindle. Continue twisting the spindle with both hands, but before it touches the floor or untwists, wind your wool onto the **spindle shaft**. It takes a lot of practice and trial and error, but with time, you'll get the hang of it!

# Breadmaking and Baking

There are lots of different ways to make bread, but many recipes follow the same basic steps to go from simple ingredients to a delicious, mouthwatering loaf.

## ◆ Breadmaking Basics ◆

**Mixing ingredients.** Most bread recipes have four main ingredients: flour, salt, water, and yeast (or another leavening agent). Many chemical reactions begin to take place as the ingredients are mixed together. Gluten is activated when combined with water and then kneaded. The leavening agent begins to produce gas bubbles. While mixing may seem like a simple step, it is vital to the success of the loaf. Mixing the ingredients must be done thoroughly to avoid any clumping, but it is important not to overmix the dough. Overmixing causes the dough to lose its elasticity and hinders the rising process later on.

**Rising.** The rising process (called *proofing*) is a time that allows fermentation to take place. As the dough is left to rest, the yeast will transform sugars into two by-products: carbon dioxide and alcohol. The carbon dioxide gas bubbles cause the dough to rise and gain volume. The alcohol simply evaporates during the baking process.

**Kneading.** This step helps to develop the dough. The folding and stretching creates stronger bonds and networks between the gluten molecules. Kneading also helps to release any larger air pockets that may have formed while the dough was rising, and it is essential for creating a dough that is consistent throughout. After this step, another round of rising and kneading may be in order, depending on the recipe.

**Baking.** This is the most transformational step in the breadmaking process. Many chemical reactions take place to transform a blob of dough into delicious bread. As heat is introduced, yeast begins to work faster, producing more carbon dioxide and alcohol. In turn, the volume of the gas expands, causing the loaf to rise even more, and the alcohol evaporates. In the oven, the bread eventually becomes so hot that the yeast dies. The crumb structure will solidify so that the bread can hold its shape.

**Cooling.** We often overlook this final step, but it is essential in maintaining the bread's structure. If you try to slice the loaf while it's still hot, it will just deflate and tear. If you wait until it's completely cool, it can be sliced without any damage or crumbling.

## • Making Your Own Sourdough Starter •

Sourdough starter is a fermented culture that is used as a leavening agent instead of yeast. The simplicity of the ingredients and steps makes sourdough a great recipe for beginning bread makers.

Sourdough starters are easy to set up and get going. It just takes time. Follow these basic instructions to start your own!

**Day 1:** Mix 60 grams of flour and 60 grams of water in a large jar and cover with a lid or plastic wrap. Put in a warm location.

**Day 2:** Check on your starter to see if there are any bubbles, which are a sign that fermentation has begun.

**Day 3:** Discard half of the starter. Add in 60 grams of flour and 60 grams of water. Mix until smooth.

**Days 4–6:** Repeat the steps from day 3. Watch as your starter begins to rise.

**Day 7:** The starter should be ready for use! If it isn't ready, continue to feed it for another week or so.

Here are some tips for maintaining your sourdough starter:

- To get started, keep the mixture in a warm, cozy location.
- If you are an infrequent baker, store the starter in the refrigerator to slow the fermentation process and have starter ready at any time.

- Feed your starter every 12 to 24 hours using the same type of flour you originally added.
- When feeding, use equal parts water and flour.
- Weight is the best measurement to use when feeding the starter since water is so much heavier than flour.
- If you aren't sure whether your starter is ready or not, drop a bit of starter into a glass of water. If it floats, it's ready to be used.

# Farmer's Sourdough Recipe

**PREP TIME:** 7 days to prepare the starter (see instructions above)

**PROOF TIME:** 3–5 hours

## WHAT YOU'LL NEED

» 4 cups bread flour, plus additional for kneading and dusting

» 1⅓ cup + 2 tablespoons water

» 2 teaspoons sea salt

» ½ cup sourdough starter

## YOU CAN DO IT!

**ADD** flour, water, salt, and sourdough starter in a bowl and mix.

**TURN OUT** dough onto a lightly floured surface and begin to knead.

**KNEAD** dough for 15–20 minutes, until it is slightly sticky and you can stretch it without tearing.

**PLACE** dough in a lightly oiled bowl. Cover bowl with a clean cloth and let the dough **PROOF** in a warm place until doubled in size (1–3 hours).

**PUNCH** down dough and roll into a ball, folding edges to center.

**LIGHTLY GREASE** your loaf pan with vegetable shortening or line a dutch oven with a sheet of parchment paper large enough to cover the bottom and sides.

**PLACE** loaf into a loaf pan or dutch oven. Cover and PROOF the dough again (1–2 hours).

Make sure you have an adult around to help with the oven.

**PREHEAT** oven to 400°F and place an empty roasting pan on the lowest rack.

**SCORE** the dough by using a sharp knife or kitchen scissors to cut simple lines into the top of the dough.

**PLACE** the uncovered loaf pan or dutch oven on the middle rack of the oven and **ADD** a pitcher of hot or boiling water into the empty roasting pan to create steam.

**BAKE** for 30–40 minutes.

**MAKES** 1 loaf

# Make Your Own Pie Crust

In addition to bread, people have been baking pies for thousands of years! The earliest pies were typically made with meat, vegetables, and potatoes and were baked over a hot fire. Today, pies are a delicious treat and are used to symbolize and celebrate holidays and special occasions.

## WHAT YOU'LL NEED

» 2 cups flour
» 1½ tablespoons sugar
» 1 teaspoon salt
» ½ cup cold butter

» 8 tablespoons butter-flavored shortening
» 1 egg, beaten
» ¼ cup ice water

## YOU CAN DO IT:

Mix together dry ingredients (flour, sugar, salt).

Cut in butter and shortening with a pastry cutter or two knives until it resembles coarse sand.

Add the beaten egg and water and mix with a spatula or wooden spoon.

Turn out dough onto a floured surface and lightly knead until the dough forms a ball.

If the dough is too wet, add flour one tablespoon at a time until the dough just holds together but is not sticky.

Cover in plastic wrap or put into a resealable bag and place in the freezer while you make the pie filling, or keep in the refrigerator if you are making a day in advance.

Makes two pie crusts.

# Apple Pie

- » zest of one lemon
- » juice of half a lemon
- » 5 pounds apples (we used Granny Smith, Gala, and Honeycrisp)
- » 1 cup brown sugar
- » ½ cup white sugar

- » ¼ cup + 1 tablespoon flour
- » pinch of salt
- » 2 teaspoons cinnamon
- » 1 teaspoon nutmeg
- » ½ teaspoon cardamom
- » 2 teaspoons vanilla extract
- » 1 chilled pie crust

## YOU CAN DO IT:

Core, peel, and slice apples.

Combine apples, sugars, flour, salt, spices, and vanilla in a large heavy bottom pan over medium heat. Make sure you have an adult to help you around the stove and oven.

Stir apples until they are at the desired softness and caramel forms to the apples (about 20 minutes).

Remove from heat and let cool to room temperature.

Heat oven to 450°F.

Drape pie crust over pie pan or cast-iron skillet.

Crimp edges if using only a bottom crust.

Pour cooled filling into pie crust. You can add a top crust or make a lattice top for decoration.

Bake for 15 minutes, then cover edges with foil and turn down the oven to 350°F. Bake for an additional 30–40 minutes.

Remove and let pie cool completely before serving.

# Cooking and Grilling Basics

Cooking in the kitchen is for everyone! Before jumping right in, there are a few things we need to discuss so that everyone stays safe.

## ✦ Kitchen Safety ✦

### Handwashing

You have probably been reminded your whole life to wash your hands, but this is very important when working in the kitchen—especially when preparing food for others to enjoy. Washing your hands with soap and warm water kills germs and bacteria. It also removes dirt. If you lick your fingers or get your hands dirty at any point during the cooking process, be sure to give them another wash.

### Knives

There are lots of sharp tools in the kitchen that are helpful for cutting, grating, and chopping. As long as you are attentive and careful around sharp objects, there should be no accidents. If a knife does slip out of your hand or off the counter, the best thing to do is let it fall. Trying to catch a falling knife will most likely lead to being cut. Instead, back away and let the knife fall to the ground, then reach down, pick it up, and rinse it off.

### Fire

When cooking and grilling, you will be using hot elements and open flames. Grease and oil fires can easily flare up if you are not careful. If a fire does pop up, do not throw water on it. Many kitchen fires will only grow bigger if water is added. Always be sure to have a fire extinguisher close by. If a fire occurs, quickly and calmly grab your fire extinguisher and remember the acronym PASS, which stands for *pull, aim, squeeze,* and *sweep*.

- **Pull:** There is a pin at the top that prevents someone from accidentally setting off the fire extinguisher. Pull this pin to remove it and prepare the extinguisher for use.
- **Aim:** Grasp the hose and aim it at the fire.
- **Squeeze:** With your other hand, slowly squeeze the trigger.
- **Sweep:** Sweep the hose from side to side across the burning area to ensure all of the fire is extinguished.

## ✦ Cooking Terms ✦

There are so many different ways to prepare food and so many different cooking terms that sometimes recipes can get confusing. Here are a few common cooking techniques and their definitions.

- **Chop:** Cut into large squares. The exact size will vary depending on the recipe.
- **Cube:** Cut into small cubes that are usually about ½ inch thick.
- **Dice:** Cut into even smaller cubes about ¼ to ⅛ inch thick.
- **Julienne:** Cut vegetables into long, thin strips about ¼ inch thick.
- **Mince:** Cut as small as possible. This is often done with fresh garlic.
- **Broil:** Food is directly introduced to dry heat. This is often done to melt cheese.
- **Braise:** The meat or vegetables are first browned in butter or oil before being cooked on low heat over a long period of time in a small amount of simmering liquid.
- **Sear:** Quickly cook meat over high heat to brown the surface and capture the juices inside.
- **Sauté:** Cooking and browning small pieces of food in oil or butter.
- **Roast:** Cooking meat or poultry in an oven with dry heat.
- **Marinate:** Allowing food, usually meat, to soak in a flavorful sauce or liquid before cooking.

# ◆ Grilling ◆

When first learning how to grill, it can be intimidating, but it is worth it! Use this list of grilling basics to help you get started.

- Always make sure there is adult supervision close by.
- Ask someone for help if you need it.
- Clean the grate to prevent food from sticking.
- Heat the grill before putting food on.
- Stay close and keep an eye on what you are grilling.
- Oil burns away under high heat, so oil the food rather than the grate.
- Season food ahead of time to allow the flavors to settle in.
- Don't use the same plate for raw meat as cooked meat. Get a clean plate for cooked food.
- Cook vegetables, fruits, and delicate meats such as fish and chicken over lower heat.
- Flare-ups will happen when grilling. Don't panic, but do be careful.
- Move the food around the grill surface to take advantage of the different temperatures and space.

# Blueberry Dutch Pancakes

Here's one of our favorite weekend breakfasts on the ranch!

## WHAT YOU'LL NEED

» 4 farm-fresh eggs
» ¾ cup whole milk
» ½ teaspoon vanilla extract
» 2 tablespoons sugar
» ¾ cup all-purpose flour, sifted
» pinch of kosher salt

» ½ teaspoon lemon or orange zest
» 2 tablespoons butter, melted
» 1 tablespoon lard or vegetable shortening
» ½ cup fresh blueberries

## YOU CAN DO IT!

Preheat the oven to 450°F. Make sure you have an adult nearby to help with the oven.

In a bowl, combine eggs, milk, and vanilla.

In a separate bowl, mix together the sugar, flour, salt, and lemon or orange zest. Add the dry ingredients to the wet ingredients and mix. Stir in the melted butter until just combined.

Let the batter rest in the refrigerator for 10 minutes.

In the meantime, put a 12-inch cast-iron pan in the oven to preheat. After a few minutes, remove the pan from the oven and add the lard to melt.

Add the batter into the pan and sprinkle with blueberries.

Bake in the cast-iron pan at 450°F for 15–20 minutes. Enjoy!

# How to Make Scrambled Eggs

» eggs (2 per person)   » salt
» butter   » milk

## YOU CAN DO IT!

We're going to teach you how to make scrambled eggs so you can try making them for your parents, siblings, or friends.

You start with some eggs. If you have chickens, you can collect the eggs fresh from them! Before you get started, you will need a bowl to crack the eggs in and a good frying pan or skillet.

To crack an egg, hit it once against the rim of the bowl so the shell cracks. Hold the egg over the bowl, put your thumb in to open it all the way so it empties into the bowl. Try to make sure no shell gets in there. When you live on a farm, it's always good to crack your eggs in a bowl first in case you get a yucky one. If they are farm-fresh eggs, the yolks will be deep yellow.

Make sure you have an adult to help you around the stove. Melt three pats of butter in a pan. While the butter is melting, break the egg yolks and whisk the eggs in the bowl. Add a little bit of milk and whisk some more. Make sure the pan is nice and hot and pour in the egg mixture. Keep mixing in the pan so nothing sticks to the bottom. Turn down the temperature if the eggs start to stick too much. Keep mixing.

Now turn off the heat. Some people like their eggs firmer and others like them more runny, so adjust cooking time to get the consistency you want. Don't add salt to your eggs until they are done or else they won't taste as good. Save the salt until the end.

You can serve the scrambled eggs on toast or top them with cheese, avocado, and tomatoes . . . or just enjoy them with a dash of salt!

# Cowboy Chili

I've adapted this recipe from the version in my first cookbook, *Five Marys Ranch Raised*.

One of my absolute favorite meals to make is a big pot of chili. Make it on a Sunday to have leftovers throughout the week, or make it when you need to feed a crowd. Enjoy a bowl on its own, or serve it over mac-n-cheese, chili dogs, thick-cut french fries . . . you name it!

Follow this exact recipe or experiment a bit with your favorite spices and toppings. Makes 6–8 servings.

## WHAT YOU'LL NEED

» ¼ cup chili powder
» 1 teaspoon ground cumin
» 1 teaspoon ground coriander
» 1 teaspoon oregano
» 1 teaspoon smoked paprika
» ½ teaspoon garlic powder
» ½ teaspoon cayenne
» 1 teaspoon kosher salt
» ½ teaspoon black pepper
» 2 tablespoons extra-virgin olive oil
» 1 medium yellow onion, finely chopped
» 1 medium red bell pepper, diced
» 1 small green bell pepper, diced

» 2 pounds ground beef, preferably chuck or sirloin
» 1 (15-ounce) can pinto beans, rinsed and drained
» 1 (15-ounce) can kidney beans, rinsed and drained
» 1 (15-ounce) can diced tomatoes
» 1 cup beef broth

### For serving (optional):

» shredded cheddar cheese
» sour cream
» chopped green onions
» avocado
» your favorite bread rolls

## YOU CAN DO IT:

In a small bowl, combine the first nine ingredients and set aside.

Make sure you have an adult nearby to help with the stove. Heat olive oil in a large pot over medium heat. Add onion and bell peppers and cook for 7–8 minutes or until veggies are soft and start to brown.

Turn heat to medium-high and add the ground beef. Cook until it is no longer pink, about 5 minutes.

Add the beans, diced tomatoes, beef broth, and combined seasonings to the pot and stir.

When the chili begins to boil, reduce the heat to low. Cook, stirring occasionally, for about an hour or until the chili feels thick.

If you want the chili to be a little bit thinner, just add more beef broth or water. Scoop some chili into a bowl and add your favorite toppings . . . enjoy!

# The Perfect Steak

## PREPPING TIPS

Thaw meat overnight in the refrigerator.

Let the steak come to room temperature before cooking.

Season your steak ahead of time.

Make sure your grill or pan is really hot.

## ON THE STOVE OR IN THE OVEN

Preheat oven to 500°F. Heat a cast-iron pan on the stove for 5 minutes on high.

Place seasoned, room-temperature steak into the pan and sear for 30 seconds on each side.

Place into the 500°F oven until internal temperature reaches 5 degrees below the temperature for your desired doneness (see "Degrees of Doneness"). Remove from the pan and let rest for 10 minutes under tented foil.

## ON THE GRILL

Light charcoal or gas grill and wait at least 10 minutes for the grill to fully heat up.

Place seasoned, room-temperature steak on the grill over an open flame. For optimal grill marks, try not to move the steak around!

After 3 minutes flip the steak. Cook the second side for an additional 2–3 minutes. Depending on how close you are to desired doneness, leave the steak over the flame or move to a cooler section of the grill.

When the internal temperature of the steak reaches 5 degrees below the temperature for desired doneness, remove from the grill and let rest for 10 minutes under tented foil.

# Degrees of Doneness

Using a meat thermometer is the best way to achieve your desired doneness.

**Rare:** 125°–130° (cool red center)

**Medium-Rare:** 135°–140° (cool pink center)

**Medium:** 145°–150° (warm pink center)

**Medium-Well:** 150°–155° (slightly pink center)

**Well Done:** 155°–160° (no pink)

# Candlemaking

**B**eeswax is a common material for making candles. Many people prefer it over other waxes because of its natural scent, high melting point, bright burn, and environmental friendliness. Beeswax does not require chemical processing and is a natural by-product of the beekeeping industry. It's a substance made by bees that they use to store honey and raise their broods. Beeswax has a natural, subtle scent of honey and nectar. Unlike other candles, beeswax emits light similar to the light spectrum of sunlight—bright and warm-toned. This is because of its high melting point of about 150°F.

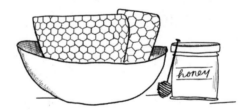

## ◆ Make a Pair of Beeswax Taper Candles ◆

**Supplies:** 1 (8×16-inch) sheet of beeswax, 2 candle wicks (metal free), scissors, and a ruler

1. Measure and cut your beeswax sheet in half, creating two 8×8 squares.
2. Place the wick (we used square braid cotton) along the bottom edge of one square, leaving about half an inch extra on each side.
3. Start to gently cover the wick with the beeswax sheet. If the wax begins to crack, you'll need to warm it up with a hair dryer for about 30 seconds on low.
4. Once you have the wick covered, begin to tightly roll the beeswax sheet, making sure the base and top edges remain even.
5. Use your fingernail to gently press or smear the final edge into the rest of the candle.
6. Trim the wick at the bottom and firmly press it into the bottom of the candle.
7. Repeat steps 2–6 for the other beeswax square.
8. Trim the tops of the wicks to about ¼ inch and enjoy!

# Leatherwork

### ◆ Step-by-Step Leather Patch ◆

**Materials:** cutting board (or poundo board), mallet, sharp pair of scissors, X-Acto knife, transfer paper, stenciling tool, edger, drafting compass, swivel blade knife, jeweler's rouge, clear ruler, lead pencil, charcoal pencil, leather stamps, gel antique, protective eyewear, nitrile gloves, leather finish (Tan-Kote), cloth rags, water, dauber, leather cement

1. Draw your design on transfer paper with charcoal pencil.

2. Using an X-Acto knife, leathercraft knife, or sharp heavy-duty scissors, cut a piece of leather to the desired shape and size for your patch and spray it with water.

3. Transfer the design onto the leather with lead pencil.

4. Use stencil tool to carve design.

5. Use a beveling tool to round off the edges on your piece of leather.

6. Stamp leather as desired.

7. Apply a small amount of gel antique to a dauber and apply to your design. (Wear gloves for this step!)

8. Clean up any excess gel antique from the leather with a rag. (Don't press too hard!)

9. Place the Tan-Kote on top (moving in little circles).

10. Let the Tan-Kote set, and dab with a rag if there are any big pools.

11. When your finished product dries it will get stiffer. Give it a final rubdown with an old cloth and make sure to get into all the little creases.

If you are adding your leather patch to an object like a hat, apply a thin coat of leather cement on the back of the patch and apply it anywhere on the hat you'd like!

# How to Make Maple Syrup

## ◆ How to Identify a Maple Tree ◆

Maple syrup comes from maple trees! The most ideal kind of maple tree is a sugar maple. But before you can tap sugar maple trees, you first have to identify them. However, when it's time to tap the trees in late winter, they usually don't have any leaves. So people who harvest maple sap must identify their trees in the summer or fall when the trees still have leaves on them.

To identify sugar maple trees, look for a few specific details.

**Leaves.** Maple leaves have some distinct characteristics. First, they are 3 to 5 inches in length and width. Second, they are usually dark green with light green on the underside of the leaf. In the fall, however, they can turn bright orange, yellow, or red! Third, maple leaves have five "lobes," or pointed sections, with U-shaped notches in between. Fourth, they have three primary veins that lead from the stem to the three top lobes. If you have maple trees in your backyard, compare them to this diagram. Do you have a sugar maple or a different variety?

**Fruit.** Another thing to look for on maple trees is their fruit. Now, it's not the kind of fruit that you can eat, but rather the pair of seeds (called *samaras* or *keys*) that develop from the small flowers of maple trees. The seeds are only visible in the late summer and early autumn.

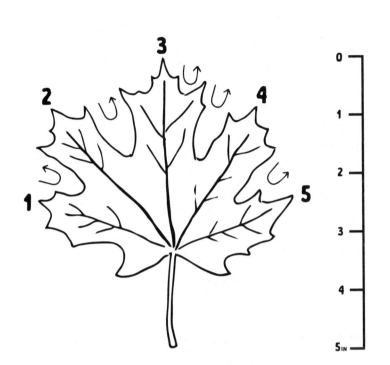

They are bright lime green and turn brown before they fall off the tree. The keys are about one inch long. When they fall, they look like little helicopters as they spin to the ground.

**Bark.** It's difficult to identify a sugar maple by its bark because it can vary from tree to tree. However, sugar maples generally have gray-brown bark when they are young and dark brown bark when they are mature.

**Tree shape.** When covered in leaves in the summer and fall, sugar maple trees are oval shaped. Their branches point toward the sky, with the bottom branches sweeping upward and the top branches standing straight up.

### • Making Maple Syrup •

#### Drilling

The first step is to get out into the woods to drill holes for taps called spiles. Picking a spot to drill can be one of the trickiest things to do. Old holes are considered to be a healing wound on the tree, so it is important to find a new drilling location each time.

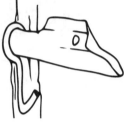

After a hole has been drilled in about an inch, it will be ready for a spile, which acts as a slide for the sap to run out. Attach a bucket or bag to the hook on the spile to collect the liquid.

#### Collecting

As the sun shines and the days warm, the sap will begin to trickle out of the trees. It may not seem like much comes out, but in a good, solid season, one tap will average ten to fourteen gallons of sap. Empty the buckets or bags into a larger collection barrel until it's time to cook the sap.

#### Cooking

Sap creates a LOT of steam, so it's best to cook it outside or in your garage, not in the kitchen. Have an adult help you with this project.

Choose a wide pan or dutch oven to use. Pour sap into the pot and set it on the heat source—you can use an outdoor propane burner or camp stove. Bring the sap to a boil. As the water evaporates, make sure to always keep a few inches of sap in the pot. Continue adding sap as it boils down.

Once the water in the sap is boiled off, you will have maple syrup. Maple syrup boils at a higher temperature than water. Using a candy thermometer, check to see if the temperature is 7.1 degrees above boiling (about 218°F).

You can set up a large pot on the stove for a small batch, but you still want to make sure to consider the sticky, sappy steam it produces.

# Simple Sewing Fixes

**H**and sewing has been around since the beginning of time and is still an incredibly useful skill to have today. Hand sewing can be used for simple projects like securing a button, patching a hole, and mending a tear. It can also be used for embroidering complicated or intricate designs. No matter your skill level, you only need a few simple tools for a hand sewing project. Materials you will need for hand sewing include fabric, a needle, a thimble, and thread. Other helpful items to have are scissors or a rotary cutter, a pin cushion and pins, measuring tape, a seam ripper, an iron, and binder clips.

Not all hand sewing is the same, and there are several different types of stitches. A stitch refers to a single turn or loop of thread or yarn.

## ◆ How to Sew on a Button ◆

Knowing how to sew on a button is an important skill—especially when you're in a pinch! Flat buttons with two or four holes are the most common type. To begin, thread your needle with a good amount of thread (about 24 inches is great).

Pass your thread through the needle's eye so that the thread is doubled up, then secure it on the needle by tying the two ends in a knot. Lay the fabric down flat and push the needle from back to front exactly where you want your button to go. Pull the thread all the way through until you reach the knot, which should be on the inside of the garment.

Place the button on the needle (any hole is fine) and guide your needle through another hole of the button. Repeat this several times until your button feels secure. When you're finished, secure the thread and button by threading your needle through the button one last time and creating a loose stitch on the inside of your fabric. Pass the needle through the loop and secure with a knot. Trim away any extra thread.

# ◆ How to Sew a Hem ◆

The last step in most sewing projects is to sew a hem. Sewing a hem refers to finishing the rough edge of your fabric to prevent it from fraying. A hem can also be used to adjust the length of your garment. You can sew a hem either by hand or with a machine.

To sew a hem by hand, first measure and fold the fabric to its desired length. (Make sure the edge is straight!) Use an iron to flatten it. Use pins to secure the fold in place.

Thread a needle with your desired thread color. Starting at one end of the fabric, make two stitches in the same place without pulling the thread all the way through. Pass the needle through the loop and pull to tighten your knot on the fabric. Pull just hard enough to secure the thread, but don't allow the fabric to bunch.

Pass your needle and thread through your fabric using a cross stitch. This is a crisscross formation of the thread, creating an X shape. When you reach the end of the hem, tie a knot in the same way that you started. Trim away any extra thread.

## ◆ How to Mend a Tear Using a Patch ◆

If you're doing any kind of exploring, adventuring, or working (which you definitely are if you're reading this book!), you're bound to collect some tears in your clothes. Knowing how to mend them is a great way to make those clothes last longer, and it's a practical place to start learning how to sew.

Let's say you find a hole in your pant leg. This is very common and can be fixed with a patch, needle, and thread . . . no machine needed! Patches often add character to your clothes, so you can pick a fabric that blends in well or something that stands out to add some flair.

First, cut away some of the longer loose threads around the tear. You can place your patch on either the inside or outside of your pant leg. In this tutorial, we'll be placing the patch on the inside of your jeans.

Use scissors or a rotary cutter to cut a piece of fabric a little bit larger than the hole you are covering. Iron the fabric to remove any wrinkles so it will lay flat. Place the patch over the hole and begin sewing from the inside of the pant leg so the knot is on the inside where no one can see it. Sew around the edge of the hole using a crisscross pattern. When finished, tie off the thread on the inside of your pant leg.

# Create an Irrigation System

This project is an ancient irrigation system that uses a porous clay pot to slowly release moisture into the soil. Plant roots grow toward the pot so the plant can drink as much water as it needs.

### ◆ Materials ◆

- Trowel
- 1 terra-cotta clay pot (unglazed) with a drainage hole
- 1 terra-cotta clay saucer (also unglazed), same diameter as the top of the pot
- Waterproof, expanding permanent glue
- Small rock, larger than the pot's drainage hole
- A skinny stick

*Note: If you live in a really dry, arid location, use a larger pot. Buy smaller pots if you live in a moist or wet location.*

### ◆ Directions ◆

**1.** Do a little science experiment to make sure your terra-cotta pot is porous. Fill up the pot with water and let it sit for an hour. You want the outside of the pot to be damp after letting it sit. If it is not, this may indicate an imperfection. Your pot will not work for this project if it is not damp after an hour.

2. Make sure the rim of the saucer is dry. Follow the package instructions to apply glue to the rim of the saucer. Now place the mouth of the pot on the rim of the saucer so the two pieces are glued together.

3. Give the pot time to dry. You can place a heavy object on top to help cement the two pieces together.

4. Once dry, check for any gaps. Fill them in with more glue. Set the pot to dry overnight.

5. Dig a hole in your garden a little larger than the pot. Place the pot in the hole with its drainage hole facing up. Fill in around the pot with dirt, leaving about one inch of the pot exposed above the soil line. Plant new plants or seedlings a few inches away from the pot. If there are already plants in your garden, dig the hole about six inches away from the base of the plants to avoid damaging the roots.

6. Fill the pot with water. You can use a single-spouted watering can or a hose.

7. Place the small rock over the drainage hole to reduce evaporation. Add your own flair to the rock by painting it with acrylic paint!

8. Monitor your new irrigation system. Place the skinny stick in the drainage hole. You will be able to tell how full it is by seeing what portion of the stick comes back damp. Add water as needed.

# Four Important Knots to Know

**T**o practice your knots, find a rope or line that is not too thin, not too thick—something that feels easy to work with in your hands.

As you learn the knots, think about one end of your line as the working end and the other as the standing string. That will help you know which way to go to make the knot.

### ◆ Figure Eight Knot ◆

The figure eight knot is a secure stopper knot. Climbers and sailors use this knot to prevent ropes from sliding out of the rigging, but it is commonly used in jewelry making and decorating as well.

Place your string in a horizontal line. The right side will be the working end. Make a loop with the working end hanging over the standing string. Wrap the working end under the line, then through the open loop, and pull to tighten.

## ✦ Halter Hitch ✦

In working with horses, we always use quick-release knots like the halter hitch. That's because when a horse is tied up, they'll sometimes pull back their heads or back up really hard. When they do that, you want to be able to release the rope quickly so they don't hurt themselves, the fence, or the rope. With this type of knot, you'll be able to release the knot with a single pull.

To tie a halter hitch, make a "4" shape with the horizontal line on top of the vertical line. The end of the horizontal line is your working end. Bring the working end behind the 4 loop. Make another loop with the working end, and bring it through the open 4 loop space. Then pull tight.

If that part of the rope is tight and the horse pulls backward, it's not going anywhere. The horse will not be running off into the great unknown! But if you simply pull the end of the rope, it will release in one swift motion.

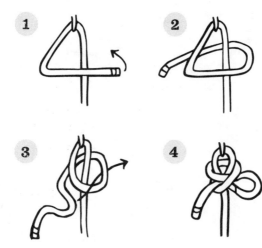

## ✦ Butcher's Knot ✦

The butcher's knot is mainly used to prepare meat for roasting. Tying the meat helps it to retain its shape while it is being cooked. The string used for tying meat is made from cotton and is oven safe. It's commonly referred to as butcher's twine, cooking twine, or kitchen twine. It's been used for ages since it is highly durable and inexpensive.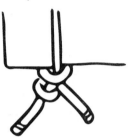

A butcher's knot is basically a slipknot, which means you can adjust it very easily after you tie it. There's no need to hold the knot in place to tighten it.

To make a butcher's knot, wrap the twine or cord around the roast (or whatever object you're working with). With the working end of the string, loop around and over the standing string and pass the working end through the loop. Then make a second loop with the standing string and pass the working end through the second loop. Pull that end tightly and you'll have your butcher's knot!

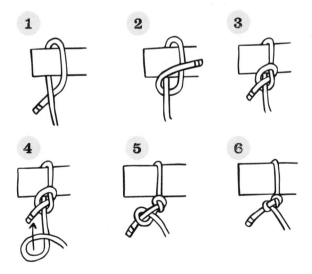

# ◆ Bowline ◆

The great thing about the bowline knot is that it is both easy to tie and easy to loosen. This is important when there's a lot of tension on the rope, like in towing and rescue situations and sailing. For example, when using a truck or tractor to pull a car out of the mud, this is the knot to use for the tow rope!

Start by making a loop with the working end of the rope on top of the standing string. Pass the working end through the loop, bring it around behind the standing string, and then bring it back through the loop a second time. You'll notice the rope is entering and exiting the loop at the same time. Pull it tight and you have a bowline!

The bowline is a very secure knot that will stay tied as you're towing things. But no matter how tight you pull it, a bowline will still be easy to untie once you're done.

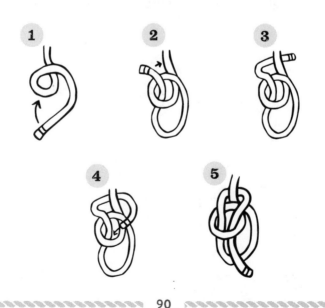

Part 3

# ANIMALS

# Horses

# ✦ How to Groom a Horse ✦

Horses that are kept in stables should be groomed regularly, but horses that stay out in the pasture do not need to be groomed as often. This is because horses in the pasture groom themselves naturally by rolling in grass, scratching on trees, and nuzzling each other.

To begin grooming your horse, first tie them up with a halter and lead using a quick-release knot such as a halter hitch. Start by picking your horse's hooves. Grab the hoof pick in one hand and slide your other hand down the horse's leg, placing pressure with your fingers near their fetlock to cue them to pick up their foot. Pick and brush out all the dirt around the frog of the hoof and around the shoe if needed. Picking your horse's feet regularly is very important for their health.

For the body of your horse, start with using a curry comb over the whole body to loosen up any stubborn dirt or mud. Metal or rubber curry combs work best for this part because of their stiffness. Work from the neck to the hindquarters on each side of the horse, using long strokes in the direction of hair growth.

Once all the dirt is loose, move to the dandy brush. This is a hard bristled brush that works well to get the dirt and dust out of the hair. Work down the sides of the horse using a flicking motion with your hand, and don't forget the legs.

Now move on to the body brush or soft brush. Because of its softness, this works especially well for the horse's head but can be used over the whole body. Use this brush to clean the horse's face; if needed, use a damp washcloth to clean around the eyes and nose. Then use it to brush the rest of the horse's body and legs.

Finally, use a wide-tooth mane comb to brush through the horse's mane and tail. If there are stubborn tangles, using a detangler spray can help. Remember to always move calmly around your horse and be aware of their movements.

## ◆ Horse Anatomy ◆

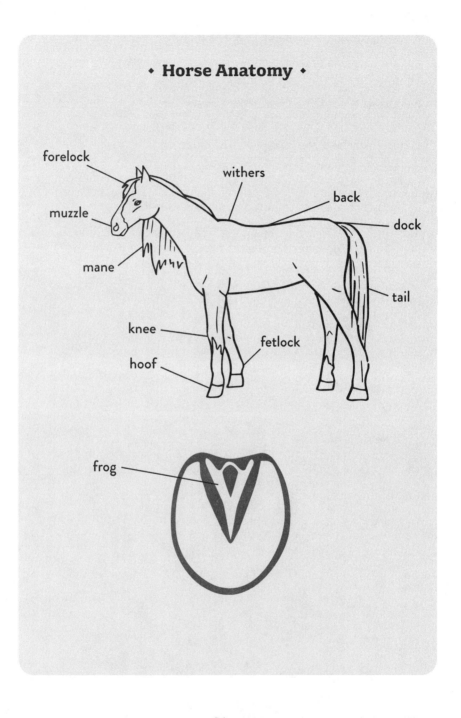

forelock

withers

back

dock

muzzle

mane

tail

knee

fetlock

hoof

frog

## ◆ Horse Breeds ◆

The following are some popular breeds of horses:

**Arabian horses** are one of the oldest known breeds. These horses tend to be on the smaller side and are noted for their high intelligence.

**Quarter horses** are popular across North America. They are commonly used to work with cattle and in competitions. They are known for their speed and agility.

**Draft horses** are known for their great strength. They have been used for centuries to pull heavy loads, and farmers once used them for plowing their fields. Examples of draft horses are Clydesdales, Belgians, and Shires.

**Rocky Mountain horses** are known for their versatility. They are great riding horses that have a lot of endurance and an easy gait.

### ✦ How to Saddle and Bridle a Horse ✦

Tie up your horse with a halter and lead, making a quick-release knot such as a halter hitch. Brush out your horse thoroughly to get rid of any dirt or mud. It is especially important to brush where the cinch or girth will be placed under the horse's belly so there is nothing rubbing between the horse and cinch. After the horse is brushed and its feet are cleaned, you may saddle the horse.

Always approach your horse from the left side. Start by placing the saddle pad in the correct position on the horse's back. It should be centered between the withers and hindquarters. Then gently place your saddle on top of the saddle pad. Make sure the saddle is centered and fitted properly.

The latigo is a strip of leather that is attached to a D-ring (a ring shaped like the letter D) on the saddle that then runs through the opening of the cinch to connect them.

Run the latigo through the front cinch and pull until it fits snugly against the horse but not too tight. Then pull up the back cinch doing the same thing. If you are using a breast collar, attach it now. This process could be different depending on whether you prefer English or Western style riding. English saddles do not have a back cinch but sometimes have a breast collar. After the horse is saddled, it is time to put on its bridle.

Untie the horse's lead rope, then unbuckle the halter and place it loosely around the horse's neck. This will prevent the horse from walking away. Hold the bridle in your left hand and place your right hand on top of the horse's head. Slowly bring the bridle toward the horse's mouth and transfer the bridle to your right hand. Using your left hand, guide the bit into the horse's mouth while pulling the bridle over the horse's ears. If needed, connect the chin strap securely. Now you may take the halter off the horse's neck.

### ◆ How to Mount and Dismount a Horse ◆

As always, safety should be a top priority! Always wear an equestrian helmet while riding a horse to protect you in case of a fall.

To prepare for mounting a horse, approach the horse on its left side. This is the side you mount from. Before mounting, the tack being used should be checked to ensure safety. To do this, check that the saddle pad or blanket is in the correct position under the saddle. Next, pull on the cinch or girth to make sure it is not loose. Your fingers should be able to fit snugly between the cinch and the belly of the horse. Then check that the reins are fully secured from the bit and hang over the neck of the horse.

Since there are two styles of riding horses, Western and English, there are different methods for each. To mount a horse that is being ridden English style, position your horse next to a mounting block on its left side. Step to the top of the mounting block with the reins in your left hand. Once on top, place your left hand with reins on the neck of the horse in front of the pommel (front of English saddle). Put your left foot in the stirrup—the ball of your foot should be centered on the base of the stirrup. Place your right hand on the middle of the saddle seat so that you are now facing your horse. Put pressure in your right hand on the saddle as you bounce your right foot off the block and swing your leg over the horse. Be sure to not kick your horse on the swing over. Sit gently in the seat and place your right foot in the right stirrup. Your right hand will come up to hold the reins with your left hand.

To mount your horse with Western tack, approach from the left side as you would do with English style. A mounting block is not absolutely necessary when riding Western style because the saddle has a horn whereas the English saddle does not. After the tack has been checked and is secure, hold the reins in your left hand and hold them next to the horn. Put your left foot in the left stirrup, grab the horn of the saddle with your left hand while keeping hold of the reins, and grasp the cantle (high back part of the saddle seat) with your right hand. Bounce your right foot off the ground and swing over the horse. Make sure to bounce and swing in one motion; you should not be pulling yourself up. Sit gently in the seat and place your right foot in the stirrup.

For dismounting English style, place the reins in your left hand and put your right hand on the pommel while taking both feet out of the stirrups. Leaning your body forward toward the horse's ears, swing your right leg over the horse's back. As this leg swings over, push off with your hands and slide down the side of the horse. You should land on both feet and facing your horse. Always dismount on the left side.

To dismount Western style, place the reins in your left hand and take your right foot out of the stirrup. Swing your right leg over the horse's back, leaving your left foot in the stirrup. As you come down off the horse, you may grab the horn or the cantle with your right hand for support. Your right foot will hit the ground and then you can take your left foot out of the stirrup to place on the ground.

# Chickens

# ◆ Taking Care of Chickens ◆

There are almost a hundred different breeds of chickens, and there are more chickens on Earth than any other bird. The various breeds are raised for either meat or eggs but very rarely for both. On the farm chickens can live six to ten years.

Chickens are omnivores, meaning that they eat both plants and animals. Most will feed on small insects along with grains or any chicken feed they are given. If a hen is unsatisfied with her diet, she may sometimes resort to eating her own eggs. Chickens will eat almost anything you give them from your scrap pile except citrus peels and watermelon rinds. Just be aware that green potato skins, rotten food, onions, and junk food are not good for chickens. There are still many other things you can feed them though!

Chickens are a fairly easy animal to raise and care for. Most local feed supply stores will have chicks for sale in the spring. There are also many online options that will send the chicks by mail. The same feed stores will also have all the necessary supplies for raising chicks. Be sure to purchase nutritious chick feed and a waterer. Chickens need a calcium-rich diet to produce strong eggshells. If they do not get enough calcium, the eggshells may be weak and break easily.

While many people begin raising chicks indoors, these little birds grow quickly and will soon need to be relocated. For backyard chickens, most people will opt for a chicken coop that is fenced in and covered. This will hopefully protect young chickens from any predators.

Chicken coops can be bought or built, depending on your preferences.

It only takes about 26 hours for a hen to produce an egg, and she will begin to produce the next egg 40 to 60 minutes after laying her last. On average, a chicken will lay one egg a day. Occasionally there will be a day where a hen doesn't lay an egg. Chickens also have a period of "molting" where they shed feathers to grow new ones, reduce their feed intake, and decrease their egg production. Molting is regulated by the hours of daylight and will happen during the fall and winter months. Some farmers will simulate longer days by putting lights in the chickens' nesting areas.

Chicken eggs have a permeable shell. This means that air can pass through the hard exterior. As a chick develops inside, it uses oxygen trapped in a membrane called the air sac. As the chick exhales, the air sac fills with carbon dioxide. The permeable shell allows the carbon dioxide to escape and be replaced by additional oxygen.

Chickens produce the most eggs within their first year of laying. They will begin to produce eggs when they are about 18 to 24 weeks old and will continue to lay as long as they are in good health. The health of the hen will also affect the health of the egg. As chickens grow older, they will lay larger but fewer eggs than when they were younger.

# ◆ How to Gather Eggs ◆

Roosters will fertilize eggs, but hens will lay eggs regardless of whether there are roosters around or not. Both fertilized and unfertilized eggs are perfectly safe to eat. The only difference is that an unfertilized egg will never develop into a chick. If you do have roosters and hope to raise baby chicks, go ahead and leave the eggs in the coop. The hens will know just what to do to take care of them on their own!

If you plan to collect fresh eggs for eating, be sure to collect about once a day or every other day. A hen needs to nest on an egg for 72 hours (called a "broody" hen) before the yolk starts to develop into an embryo. So if you leave eggs in the coop for several days, there is a good chance that they will become inedible. There's nothing worse than a spoiled egg in the mix when you're back in the kitchen!

When you have your eggs collected and want to ensure that they are fresh, do this simple test. Fill a glass or small bucket with water and place an egg in it. If the egg sinks, especially on its side . . . it's fresh! If the egg sinks but stands on end, it will be perfect to hard boil and will be easy to peel. If the egg floats, that is a strong indicator that it has gone bad and should not be eaten. Rotten eggs also feel a bit lighter than fresh eggs because of the air that passes through the permeable shell.

When the eggs you've collected from the coop come out clean, you don't need to worry about washing them off. Eggs have a natural coating called a "bloom" that keeps bacteria from entering through the shell. The bloom is slightly wet and glossy but dries almost instantly. Depending on the temperature and humidity of your kitchen, you can potentially leave those eggs on the counter for several weeks.

Sometimes when you collect eggs you'll find a few that are dirty and you'll want to wash them off. We just use warm water and a little bit of soap to gently wipe them clean. When you do this, you'll need to refrigerate them afterward since they will have lost their natural antibacterial properties.

# ◆ Chicken Breeds ◆

Austrolorp

Brahma

Cornish

Dominique

ISA Brown

Jersey Giant

Kadaknath

Onagadori

Polish

Quechua

Uzura-Chabo

Vorwerk

Wynadotte

Easter Egger      Frizzle      Golden Comet      Hamburg

Lavender Orpington    Mottled Houdan    Naked Neck

Rhode Island Red      Silkie      Thai Game Chicken

iXworth      Yokohama      Zottegem

# Cattle

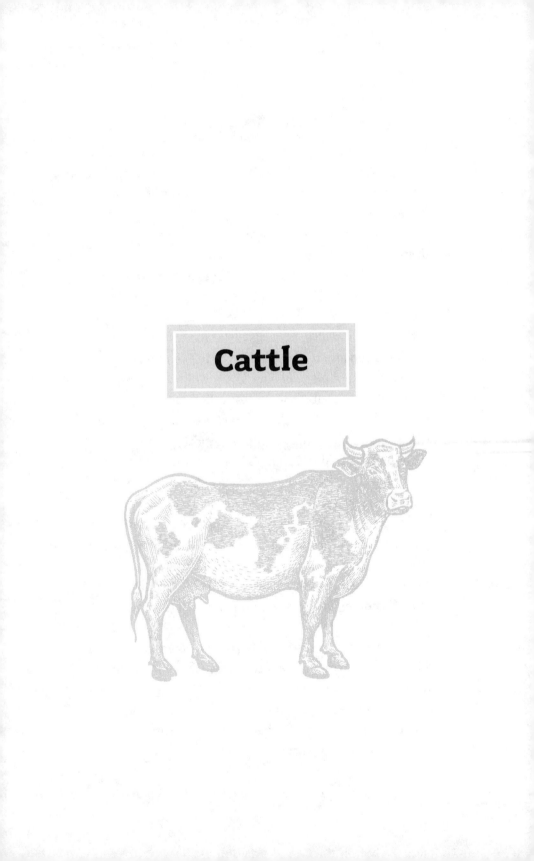

## • Cattle Care Basics •

When taking care of cattle, being calm is really important. You don't want your animals to be stressed, and you want whoever's handling the animals to be safe. Safety is always important.

When feeding cattle, remember this saying: *Grass doesn't grow year-round!* Every area of a ranch has a growing season, and cattle are only able to graze when the grass is growing. Once the grass stops growing and they are no longer able to graze for food, cattle need to be fed with something else. For us at Five Marys Farms, it is a locally raised alfalfa twice a day for the rest of the year.

An important piece of equipment when caring for cattle is a silencer chute (sometimes called a *squeeze*), which handles all sizes of cattle. It operates using hydraulics, which allows everything to move smoothly. The squeeze is designed so that the animals feel safe and comfortable. There are all sorts of reasons for bringing an animal into the silencer chute.

For one, the chute allows for organized and efficient yearly health vaccinations. The side panels allow you to inject a vaccine into the animal's neck—the ideal place for an injection. A scale is under the chute, so while the animal is being vaccinated, you can record their exact weight.

You can also use the squeeze to preg-check an animal, which refers to manually determining the animal's pregnancy status. You can use an ultrasound machine for this, but most farmers and ranchers do it the old-fashioned way by inserting a gloved hand into the cavity to check if that cow is pregnant.

The silencer chute comes in handy if a cow is in labor but the calf is stuck. Just like human babies, calves can be out of position or get stuck in the birth canal. When you notice a laboring cow that is struggling out in the pasture, or if a calf gets stuck, you can calmly lead the cow out of the pasture and into the squeeze. This will allow you to stand behind her and help her deliver the calf.

After a cow gives birth, it's time to tag the calf. This means the calf will get an ear tag with a number that matches the mother cow. The tag is used to keep track of which calf comes from which cow. Keeping accurate records is essential to track growth and development.

An animal health shed is important for keeping the necessary supplies to take care of the animals' health. Some items you should always have on hand include

- multipurpose ointment to use on cattle or horses if they have a cut
- wound spray
- hydrogen peroxide, which is often used on the ranch to disinfect a wound or to clean the surface of an animal
- lubricants if you have to reach in and pull a calf or a piglet
- syringes of varying gauge and length for the different thicknesses of each animal's skin

Vaccines prevent things like pneumonia, respiratory illness, and tetanus. Probiotics are also used to prevent illness before it happens. When you're vaccinating a lot of animals at once, you have to be sure to dispense the correct dose of vaccine for every animal.

Make sure to balance the cattle's mineral intake and administer minerals that may be lacking from their natural environment. Where we live in Northern California, and most of the American West, is deficient in selenium. Without this trace mineral at birth, an animal might not develop correctly. Just a small amount of a mineral like selenium can make the difference between life or death for animals.

# ◆ Cattle Terms ◆

- **Bovine:** An animal of the cattle group.
- **Bull:** An uncastrated male bovine that is used for breeding purposes.
- **Calf:** The male or female offspring of a cow.
- **Cow:** A mature female bovine that has had at least one calf. After giving birth to her first calf, a heifer becomes a cow.
- **Dry cow:** A cow that is not producing milk during the seven to nine months while it is pregnant.
- **Fresh cow:** A cow that has recently given birth to a calf.
- **Heifer:** A young female cow that has not had any offspring.
- **Springer:** A cow or heifer close to calving.
- **Steer:** A castrated male bovine that is primarily raised for beef.
- **Wet cow:** A cow that is currently producing milk.
- **Yearling:** A calf that is one year old.

# ✦ Cattle Anatomy ✦

### *Beef Cattle Anatomy*

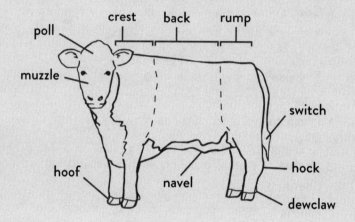

poll • crest • back • rump
muzzle • switch • hoof • navel • hock • dewclaw

### *Dairy Cattle Anatomy*

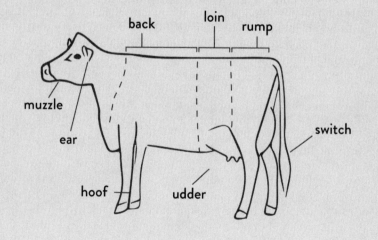

back • loin • rump
muzzle • ear • hoof • udder • switch

# • Common Cattle Breeds •

Common types of dairy cattle in the United States are Ayrshire, Brown Swiss, Guernsey, Holstein, Jersey, and Milking Shorthorn. The largest dairy breed in terms of number of cows is the Holstein.

The five most common types of beef cattle in the United States are Black Angus, Charolais, Hereford, Simmental, and Red Angus.

These breeds are popular because they tolerate many different climates and don't usually need much help during calving season. For the beef varieties, these breeds have large bodies and produce well-marbled, flavorful meat.

Ayrshire

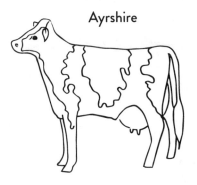

Holstein

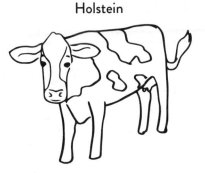

Jersey

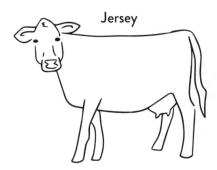

Red Angus

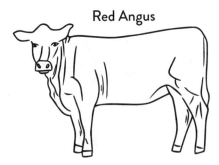

## ◆ How to Milk a Cow ◆

In order to milk a cow, first secure the animal by a halter and lead rope or put it in a confined area such as a cattle chute. Use the same method for tying a cow as for a horse. Secure the lead rope to a sturdy post using a quick-release knot such as a halter hitch. Choose a safe place for the animal in case it gets loose. If a cow is not halter broke, secure it in the cattle chute.

Begin by cleaning off the cow's udder and teats. Using a soft cloth and warm soapy water or iodine, wash the area until the skin is completely clean. This will get rid of any soils and bacteria that could contaminate the milk. Then use a clean towel to completely dry the udder. Wash your hands as well to ensure no transfer of bacteria or dirt.

Before you start the actual milking process, you need to "strip" the cow's teats. This process involves pulling down on the cow's teats multiple times to pass through

any dirt or debris that could be clogged in the milk ducts. This is done into a separate bucket placed beneath the udder so the actual milk bucket is not contaminated. Once all of the teats are stripped and there is no more discoloration of the milk, the cow is ready to be milked.

Seat yourself on a stool or squat down on the right side of the cow. You should be just ahead of the cow's back legs, not directly beside them. You should be able to move away quickly if the cow kicks or moves suddenly. Place the clean bucket on the ground under the teats to begin milking.

Place your index finger and extended thumb around one teat at the base of the udder and gently start to squeeze. The teat will fill the palm of your hand as it fills with milk. Use a downward squeezing motion to flush the milk out of the teat.

Repeat this process until that quarter of the udder is empty of milk. It will look more wrinkled and deflated than before. Continue to milk all four teats until there is no more milk. You may need to bump the cow's udder a bit to get the milk to let down. This bumping motion resembles the action of a calf and triggers a milk release.

# Sheep

# ❖ Getting to Know about Sheep ❖

Sheep are not always recognized as being special or intelligent, but this couldn't be further from the truth. They have an excellent memory! Their low maintenance care requirements make them a popular and economical animal to raise. One of the first domesticated farm animals, sheep have had a long history with humans. Their meat, wool, and milk have played vital roles in the success of many civilizations.

Here are some sheep terms you should know:

- **Dock:** A shortened tail that was cut for health reasons.
- **Ewe:** An adult female sheep.
- **Flock:** A group of sheep.
- **Gimmer:** A female sheep that has been weaned but not yet sheared, usually around 6 to 15 months old.
- **Lamb:** A baby sheep.
- **Ram:** An adult male sheep, sometimes called a buck.
- **Wether:** An adult male sheep that has been castrated.

Ram

Ewe

Lamb

Gimmer

Flock

## • Taking Care of Sheep •

When lambs are about nine months old, they are considered to be fully grown. Every night, we put down fresh straw in the barn so the ewes and lambs have a soft place to sleep. They sleep in the barn so they don't get muddy and wet at night—and that way they are safe from predators like coyotes too!

As we bring the flock into the barn, the ewes find their lambs by sound. The babies call "baa" and the mamas call "baa" (called bleats) and they know the sound of each other. When a mama thinks she has found the lamb that belongs to her, she smells the lamb to make sure. The ewe might then nurse before lying down. Once everyone has found each other, they settle in for the night and eventually the barn becomes quiet.

It's really important to have year-round care for sheep . . . they need vaccinations and their eyes have to be checked regularly. You can actually tell from the color of a sheep's eyes if they have a parasite that's taking nutrients from them.

When sheep live on rocky terrain, it acts like a natural file for their hooves . . . but it's important to check that their hooves aren't growing in a way that is uncomfortable for them!

If your sheep are living in a place with extreme temperature swings—freezing cold nights and warm days—you'll want to check that their noses aren't running, which could be a sign of pneumonia.

Sheep also need to be sheared. Shearing is an art that takes a lot of time to learn how to do right. It can be pretty dangerous for both the animal and the shearer if you're not trained to use those clippers! An experienced shearer knows how to position the sheep so they stay nice and calm and also how to turn the sheep, which makes the whole process go a lot smoother.

At Five Marys Farms, we shear every spring before the warmer months set in for the health, comfort, and safety of our sheep. It always feels great to have our beautiful flock shorn and ready for summer!

# ◆ Sheep Anatomy ◆

poll

rump

tail

ear

muzzle

flank

ribs

udder

hoof

dewclaw

## ✦ Common Sheep Breeds ✦

There are many popular breeds of sheep throughout the world. Like other farm animals, sheep are bred for specific purposes: meat, wool, milk, or some combination of those three.

Certain breeds are also better suited for particular climates. Among the most popular sheep breeds are Dorset, Hampshire, Katahdin, and Suffolk. At Five Marys Farms, we raise Navajo-Churro sheep. This breed is one of the oldest and most popular breeds in the United States. They can withstand extreme temperature changes and exist in harsh environments.

# ◆ How to Bottle-Feed a Lamb ◆

It's common for ewes to give birth to twins or triplets. When this happens, sometimes the mother rejects or abandons one of the lambs. In that case, the lamb becomes a bottle baby. This can also happen if a lamb is born too early or too weak and isn't able to survive outside on their own with the mama.

Right when you get the bottle baby lamb, you'll want to bring it in and sit with it by the fire to warm up.

Initially, you feed the lamb colostrum, not milk replacement, because colostrum is what newborns need. Colostrum refers to the first milk that the ewe's body produces after a lamb is born. It's thick and yellow so some people refer to it as "liquid gold"! It's very important that the newborn lamb gets colostrum in the first twenty-four hours of their life—it makes a big difference!

To make a bottle, use an empty plastic water or soda bottle and purchase Pritchard nipples or "teats" that can be screwed onto the bottle top. This is what the lambs will suck out of. Measure powdered milk replacer into the bottle, then fill it up the rest of the way with warm (not hot!) water. Then shake the bottle until the milk replacer is completely mixed in.

The lambs will be very excited to eat, so they'll start sucking on the nipple right away. Sometimes a newborn lamb won't suck right away, so you'll have to open their mouth just a little bit and squeeze the bottle for them to get started.

Lambs usually eat two to three times per day, depending on their size and age.

# Rabbits

# ⋄ Taking Care of Rabbits ⋄

Rabbits are very social animals—they like to have other rabbits and people around giving them lots of attention!

There are different ways to keep rabbits, but usually you will need some sort of hutch or cage that will keep them off the ground and give them good ventilation. The cage should be big enough so they can stand on their hind legs without hitting their head anywhere on the cage. Your bunny cage should have a litter box space and an area for resting, and it should be made out of metal or other indestructible material—rabbits love to chew things!

Speaking of chewing . . . make sure your rabbit always has access to grass hay. It's great for their health with all of its vitamins, minerals, and proteins. It also helps to keep your rabbit from chewing on other objects that you don't necessarily want it to.

When you hold your rabbit, align your arm to the side of its body and support its hind end. (They have fragile backbones.) You want their little toes sticking out behind your arm so they don't latch onto your side. Tuck your rabbit's head into your arm so they feel held and safe.

With over three hundred breeds, domesticated rabbits come in a wide variety of colors, shapes, and sizes. Even within a specific breed, markings and eye color can vary greatly. As with any other animal, rabbit breeds come with their own unique traits and characteristics.

Do your research to figure out which breed will be the most suitable for your family. For instance, some breeds require more attention, grooming, or exercise than others. Some of the most popular pet breeds include Mini Rexes, Holland Lops, Dutch Lops, Dwarf Lotos, and Mini Lops.

# ◆ **Rabbit Anatomy** ◆

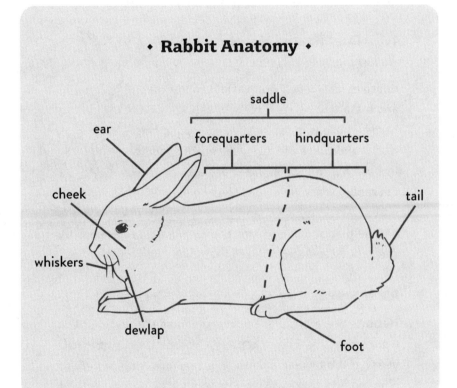

# ◆ Types of Rabbits ◆

Rabbits come in a wide variety of colors, shapes, and sizes. Wild rabbits still roam free and are different from the domesticated breeds. Rabbits raised on farms are bred for specific purposes, including meat, fur, and show. Other domestic breeds are kept as household pets.

### Wild Rabbits and Hares

Just like how our dog friends are distant relatives of wolves, domesticated bunnies are distantly related to wild rabbits and hares. These wild rabbits live all around the world, and there are many different species. In North America alone there are cotton-tail rabbits, jackrabbits, snowshoe hares, Arctic hares, Alaskan hares, and pygmy rabbits. Wild rabbits can be distinguished from the domesticated breeds by their more athletic bodies and longer, narrower heads.

### Meat Breeds

Rabbits are a popular source of meat throughout the world. They have been kept as livestock for about 1,500 years. Rabbit meat is considered a white meat similar to chicken and turkey. Many people looking to raise their own source of meat or protein will choose rabbits because they do not cost a lot of money to raise and require little space. Some of the most common meat breeds include New Zealand Whites, Californian Rabbits, American Chinchillas, and Flemish Giants.

### Fur Breeds

Breeds of Angora rabbits—including French, English, Satin, and Giant Angoras—may be raised for their fur. This fur is processed into Angora wool, which can be made into yarn and used for knitting, crocheting, and crafting just like other animal wools. Angora fur comes in a variety of colors and fiber qualities. Most Angora breeds go through a molting phase about four times a year at which times the fur is harvested and processed.

### Show Breeds

Members of youth organizations like 4-H raise rabbits for show. They are a popular animal for learning handling and showing techniques since they are relatively small. To show a rabbit in the United States, its breed must be recognized by the American Rabbit Breeders Association (ARBA). Of the over 300 domesticated breeds available, ARBA recognizes only 49. A few breeds approved for showing include the American Rabbit, Belgian Hare, Californian Rabbit, Checkered Giant Rabbit, and Dutch Rabbit.

# Working Dogs

# • Types of Working Dogs •

### Service Dogs

Service dogs are trained professionals recognized by the law. They perform specific tasks to help people who are visually impaired, deaf, or disabled. A potential service dog is first evaluated on its personality and temperament. These dogs must be calm, loyal, and intelligent. They are trained to have great focus and to ignore their impulses while on the job.

Beyond those basic requirements, service dogs receive specific training so they can help their owners with various tasks: opening doors, turning on lights, sensing health complications—even calling 911! Seeing-eye dogs guide their owners, helping them avoid dangers and locate objects. Dogs assisting the deaf can alert them to approaching traffic, the presence of another person, and other sounds. They may even be able to carry and relay messages. Needless to say, these dogs are incredibly intelligent and helpful!

Service dogs are easily identified by the vests they wear. When you see a service dog, it is important to not pet them. Always remember that they are focused and on the job!

Common breeds of service dogs include Golden Retrievers, Labrador Retrievers, and German Shepherds.

### Therapy Dogs

The main job of a therapy dog is to bring joy, cheer, and comfort to people. They work with their owners on a volunteer basis visiting hospitals, schools, nursing homes, assisted-living communities, and other places. Students, patients, and residents are allowed to inter-

act with and pet the dogs. This has proven to reduce stress and boost happiness.

Therapy dogs must be calm, friendly, and social around strangers. Therapy dogs are usually tested on behavior to make sure they do not jump on people and can walk on a loose leash.

Therapy dogs also wear a vest for identification when out on a visit, but unlike service animals you are welcome to pet these dogs.

Common breeds of therapy dogs include Golden Retrievers, Labrador Retrievers, and Cavalier King Charles Spaniels.

### Police and Military Dogs

Police and military dogs are extremely intelligent and can be trained to complete specific, complex tasks that help to solve crimes and keep people safe. They have heightened senses, strong intuition, and great athleticism.

Police dogs are trained as single-purpose or dual-purpose officers. This means that they either have a specialized job or are responsible for carrying out multiple tasks. Dogs trained in apprehending can detain dangerous suspects by biting them. Dogs trained in detection work have an incredible sense of smell to locate illegal substances, crime scene evidence, and weapons. Military dogs may also be able to sniff out landmines and other explosives.

Officers and soldiers go through the training process with the dogs they are assigned to work with. The bonds between these dogs and their handlers are known to be unbreakable.

Common dog breeds used by the police and military include Belgian Malinois, German Shepherds, Bloodhounds, Dutch Shepherds, and Labrador Retrievers.

### Search and Rescue Dogs

Search and rescue dogs are used to help to find people and save lives after natural disasters such as avalanches and earthquakes. They often work in small teams with other dogs and handlers. These dogs are able to locate people who have gotten lost or who are trapped under water, snow, or collapsed buildings. Search and rescue dogs often begin their training as puppies, learning to pick up scents and track from an early age. They are trained to work in all conditions no matter the weather.

There are many different types of tracking situations a search and rescue dog could be trained for. In general, these dogs are trained to alert their handlers when they find a missing person. Some dogs are further trained to remain with the victim and comfort them while help is on the way. Historically, Saint Bernards working in pairs have been used to locate avalanche victims. Once a victim was located, one dog would run back to guide the handler while the other would stay by the victim to keep them warm.

Common dog breeds used in search and rescue are Bloodhounds, Basset Hounds, Coonhounds, Beagles, and Saint Bernards.

### Herding Dogs

Herding dogs work with farmers to round up, herd, and protect livestock. These dogs are known for being very loyal to their owners and for having fun, distinct personalities. Their high energy levels and athleti- cism give them the ability to keep up with large livestock.

Herding dogs must also be ex- tremely intelligent. They are trained to understand a set of basic com- mands that communicate things like where to drive a herd and how fast to push them. To see if a herding dog has potential, they are introduced to livestock when they are still puppies or very young dogs.

Herding dogs can work either individually or in teams. When working in teams, dogs working from the front are often called headers or fetchers. They will repeatedly get in front of the herd to stop or turn the group. Heelers work from the back. They are responsible for driving the herd forward and making sure no animals get left behind.

Common dog breeds for herding include Australian Cattle Dogs, Australian Shepherds, Border Collies, and Bearded Collies.

### Livestock Guardian Dogs

Livestock guardian dogs are usually large dogs that protect and defend livestock. Unlike herding dogs, they live with and become members of the herd or flock. Livestock guardian dogs mark their territory throughout the property, and while this is usually enough to deter predators, they will do whatever is necessary to protect their flock. They will bark loudly to warn the flock and scare away threats, and will demonstrate aggressive behavior and even confront predators when necessary.

Common breeds that are used as livestock guardian dogs include Anatolian Shepherds, Great Pyrenees, Komondors, and Tibetan Mastiffs.

## ◆ How to Care for and Train ◆ a Working Ranch Dog

Working dogs need the same care that pet dogs need: good food, vaccinations, and regular grooming like bathing and brushing. Just like you, they need to be told when they are doing a great job. However, when a working dog is working, they should not be treated like a pet. They have a job to do.

Work with your dog every day—you want them to be your partner and have mutual respect and maintain a safe environment for all involved. It may be time-consuming, but it will definitely pay off in the long run!

Training for a livestock guardian dog is mostly instinctual. That being said, there are always more lessons for these dogs to learn. The first step is simply introducing your dog to the herd. This should happen when they are still a puppy and may start with them on a leash. If your dog acts aggressively toward the livestock, you need to continue introducing them slowly so they aren't viewed as a threat. At the same time, you do not want your livestock guardian dog to be playful with the livestock either.

Your dog will need guidance, correction, and more training until they are considered reliable at about age two. Having an older dog to model appropriate behavior can be very helpful and make the training process a little quicker and more streamlined. But remember, training livestock guardian dogs is not a one-size-fits-all job!

Part 4

# FOR YOUNG ENTREPRENEURS

# Putting Your Talents to Work!

There are so many great options to get you started with your first business and to learn the future skills you'll need to start another side business—or even a second or third business!

I've always believed in finding the most value and profit from as many avenues as it takes, seizing any opportunity I find to generate income and create a profitable business. You will learn valuable lessons from each business that will be stepping stones toward your future as an entrepreneur. Thanks to the internet, social media, and entrepreneurism, you can make almost any idea happen!

Being a small business owner and entrepreneur is a beautiful thing and a great way to live—you can be your own boss, ready to take on new challenges and seize opportunities. It's not for everyone, though. You have to learn to sell your product or service confidently, stand behind your prices, have patience with customer service issues, and always be working harder to set goals and blow past them.

Make sure that you love being an entrepreneur—that you love selling and can accept payment for your goods from people you know, which can be harder than with strangers. Make sure you have what it takes to work hard—all the time. As an entrepreneur, you don't get weekends off. You don't get to turn off your email or phone and check out (at least not easily).

If you want to be successful, you need to be willing to always be adjusting your business and making it better. It means a lot of analyzing: what you are doing, how you can improve, what direction you want to go in, where to put your resources, where to conserve, and when to keep pushing. You'll always be morphing and changing and working to achieve your goals . . . but guess what? YOU CAN DO IT!

## ◆ Selling Handmade Goods and Services ◆

When selling handmade goods, start by focusing in on one big idea. To make that big idea happen, you might need to have your irons in more than one fire, and as always . . . START SMALL!

Use the worksheets we've provided on pages 154 and 155 to calculate expenses and project profits. If you don't feel like you have a solid margin to make a profit on top of your expenses (and your time!), don't start. Keep working on your concept until your profit margin seems attractive and worth it.

### Ideas for Handmade Goods to Sell

- Flowers you grow and arrange
- Cookies or cakes you bake and decorate
- Fruits and vegetables that you grow
- Canned goods (like salsa or jam) that you make

- Handicrafts you make (like pet toys or beeswax candles)
- Stickers or prints with your drawings or paintings
- Sewn items like coin purses or tote bags
- Photography or artwork you create
- Clothing with your personal brand or a message people want to get behind
- A monthly subscription club you create and sell
- Anything you can imagine! It doesn't have to be just one!

Here are some examples of agriculture-related products that we've seen:

- Animal fat balms or skincare
- Carved antlers
- Painted cow skulls
- Yarn or felted wool
- Sheepskin rugs or cow hides
- Tallow candles
- Maple syrup
- Farm-raised honey

When selling a service, it's best to start with something you are good at or have a unique skill set for. You don't need to settle on just one service—although in the beginning one may be enough. It's great to think outside the box to find a business that you can start quickly, affordably, and without a ton of risk. That business may very well fund your dream business one day!

I love dreaming big, but I suggest starting small. You can use the "Chores and Caregiving" worksheet on page 156 as a sample worksheet for the service you decide to sell.

### Ideas for Services to Sell

- Dog walking or pet training
- Babysitting or tutoring
- Teaching lessons for a skill you love (examples: fishing, sewing, painting)
- Event planning services
- Local photography services
- Cleaning or laundry services
- Creating an online course or digital content for other businesses
- Landscaping, property management, or yardwork
- Website design

# Raising Animals for Profit

If you've never been a small business owner, take the opportunity to start small and learn to build a business . . . and to make sure you love it! You can create something now and learn from the results.

If you're interested in raising animals for profit, a great way to start small is by joining your local 4-H community! You'll learn how to handle, feed, water, groom, and show your animal all by yourself. There will be ups and downs, early mornings, late nights, hard work, and unforgettable memories. You'll work to raise your animal and then sell it at auction. It's a long process but so worth it for everything that you'll learn along the way—about yourself, agriculture, and business!

Make sure you take the time to figure out if your business idea of raising animals for profit is financially feasible for you and your family. In the big picture, margins are important. There are always going to be some unexpected or extra costs, so you need to make sure your product or service has a good margin of profit potential. You can use the "Raising Pigs for Profit" worksheet on page 157 as a guide for making your own worksheet.

You also need to make sure your price is reasonable and attractive. You know what it is worth to you . . . but is it worth that to a lot of people? Do some research. Check prices locally and online, check your competition's pricing, and make sure you aren't too far off.

You've probably heard the saying "You get out what you put in!" Nothing is more true in business. You need to put your heart and energy into it. Believe in yourself and your business idea. Start small but don't be afraid to take risks.

## ◆ Selling Eggs, Syrup, and Produce ◆

After you have been gardening or making maple syrup or raising chickens for a while, you may find that you have more produce, syrup, or eggs than you can use. You could consider selling the extra yourself! Sometimes this can be done from a small stand on the side of the road or at a farmers market. Wherever you decide to sell, be sure that you are at least making enough money to cover the production costs, such as feed for the chickens. You can create your own worksheet like the ones included in this book.

# Interesting Careers

### ✦ Veterinarians ✦

Veterinarians are vital to the health and safety of animals in agriculture. Without their work, it would be a lot harder for farmers to raise animals and keep them healthy. Vets help in maintaining the health of not only farm animals but of domesticated animals and animals living in zoos throughout the world. There are five types of veterinarians: small animal, large animal, exotic animal, specialists, and researchers. All of them have interesting work to do! Another way to work with animals is to be a trainer for working dogs—there are so many to choose from!

### ✦ Fish Hatcheries ✦

A hatchery is an enclosed, controlled environment where fish eggs are cultivated and hatched. People who work at hatcheries often send the hatchlings to fish farms where they will be raised for food or ornamental and aquarium purposes. Other hatcheries continue to raise the fish until they are juveniles and then release them into lakes, rivers, or even the ocean. This is a practice known as "fish stocking," and it helps support conservation efforts as well as commercial and recreational fishing.

## ◆ Beekeepers ◆

Beekeepers work with hives of bees, collecting honey and taking care of the hives so that they remain healthy. They have to wear protective clothing to avoid being stung!

## ◆ Welders ◆

Welding skills are highly sought after throughout many industries since it saves time and money to repair equipment on site. Welders are needed in the shipping, manufacturing, railroad, construction, automotive, and aerospace industries. Welding is also a useful skill to have in the agricultural industry. As problems come up on the ranch, creative solutions are needed. Building and implementing those ideas often requires welding.

You should not attempt welding without first having someone teach you. If you are interested in learning how to weld, be sure to check for class offerings in your area. Many high schools and community colleges offer courses for their students to learn all about welding. To learn more specialized types of welding, such as arc welding, underwater welding, laser beam welding, and ultrasonic welding, you must be specifically trained in that area. Certain colleges and universities have specialized programs to certify welders in these areas.

# ENTREPRENEUR'S WORKSHEET:
# CANDLEMAKING

## №1 INITIAL EXPENSES:

BEFORE YOU CAN BEGIN, YOU HAVE TO PURCHASE THE NECESSARY MATERIALS TO MAKE CANDLES. YOU MUST DECIDE THE SCENT, COLOR, AND TYPE OF WAX THAT YOU'RE GOING TO USE. SOME OF THESE MATERIALS YOU MIGHT ALREADY HAVE AROUND YOUR HOME!

| | |
|---|---|
| JARS | $ |
| WAX (BEESWAX, SOY, OR OTHER) | $ |
| ADD INS: ESSENTIAL OILS, OTHER FRAGRANCE, DYES | $ |
| WICKS | $ |
| THERMOMETER AND DOUBLE BOILER | $ |
| OPTIONAL: WICK BAR, WICK STICKERS, LABELS | $ |
| TOTAL | $ |

## №2 SELLING OR GIFTING:

NOW THAT YOU KNOW WHAT KIND OF CANDLES YOU'RE GOING TO MAKE, IT'S TIME TO DECIDE WHAT TO DO WITH THEM! WILL YOU KEEP THEM FOR YOURSELF, GIVE THEM AS GIFTS, OR SELL THEM? IF YOU CHOOSE TO SELL THEM, YOU NEED TO DECIDE THE SELLING PRICE FOR YOUR CANDLES:

SELLING PRICE

HOW MANY CANDLES DO YOU NEED TO SELL (INITIAL EXPENSES ÷ SELLING PRICE =TOTAL UNITS TO BREAK EVEN) IN ORDER TO PAY OFF YOUR INITIAL EXPENSES?

IF YOU CHOOSE NOT TO SELL THEM, THAT'S GREAT TOO! CANDLES ARE WONDERFUL HANDMADE GIFTS, PERFECT FOR GIFTING DURING THE HOLIDAYS OR FOR SPECIAL OCCASIONS!

# WILD EARTH DYES
## -Selling Your Handmade Goods-

## Nº1 INITIAL EXPENSES:

| | |
|---|---|
| NATURAL DYE MATERIALS (VINEGAR, VEGETABLES, FRUIT, TEA, ETC.) | $ |
| MATERIALS TO SELL : YARN, DISH CLOTHS, EGGS, ETC. | $ |
| MARKETING + PRODUCTION MATERIALS (TABLE, POTS, STORAGE BINS, ETC.) | $ |
| INITIAL CAPITAL INVESTMENT | $ |

IF YOU PLAN TO MAKE MONEY FROM SELLING YOUR DYED
CREATIONS, THE INITIAL EXPENSES PAID ARE CONSIDERED
AN INVESTMENT.

## Nº2 MONTHLY RECURRING EXPENSES:

| | |
|---|---|
| NATURAL DYE MATERIALS (AS YOU WORK THROUGH THEM) | $ |
| MATERIALS TO SELL : YARN, CLOTH, EGGS, ETC. | $ |
| MISC. (WEBSITE, FARMERS MARKET BOOTH FEE, ETC.) | $ |
| TOTAL | $ |

YOU MUST CONSIDER A FEW THINGS BEFORE YOU BEGIN:
WHO WILL YOU MARKET TO? WILL YOU SELL YOUR GOODS IN
PERSON? WHERE WILL YOU SET UP YOUR BOOTH?

## Nº3 NONRECURRING EXPENSES:

| | |
|---|---|
| BUSINESS UPGRADES AS YOU GROW (EQUIPMENT, COMPUTER PROGRAMS, ETC.) | $ |
| TOTAL | $ |

**Nº1** TOTAL **+ Nº2** TOTAL **+ Nº3** TOTAL **=** TOTAL INVESTMENT   $

# ENTREPRENEUR'S WORKSHEET:
## CHORES AND CAREGIVING

THINK ABOUT THE CHORES YOU DO AROUND YOUR HOME. WHICH OF THOSE COULD YOU USE TO EARN MONEY IN YOUR COMMUNITY? FOR EXAMPLE: BABYSITTING, RAKING LEAVES, YARD WORK, TAKING OUT THE TRASH, CUTTING WOOD, SHOVELING SNOW, DOG-WALKING, AND MORE. NEXT, THINK UP A CATCHY NAME FOR YOUR BUSINESS!

## № 1 MY BUSINESS:

DO SOME RESEARCH AND TALK TO SOME ADULTS TO FIND OUT HOW MUCH MONEY YOU CAN CHARGE FOR YOUR SERVICE. BABYSITTERS, LAWN-MOWERS, AND OTHERS USUALLY CHARGE PER HOUR, WHICH MEANS THAT YOU MAKE A CERTAIN AMOUNT OF MONEY FOR EVERY HOUR YOU WORK. HOW MUCH SHOULD YOU CHARGE PER HOUR?

## № 2 MY WAGE: $ [        ]

BEFORE YOU START, THINK ABOUT THE SUPPLIES YOU MAY NEED TO PURCHASE BEFOREHAND. FOR EXAMPLE, IF YOU'RE GOING TO RAKE LEAVES IN YOUR COMMUNITY, DO YOU NEED TO BUY A NEW RAKE? LIST YOUR INITIAL EXPENSES BELOW.

## № 3 MY INITIAL EXPENSES:

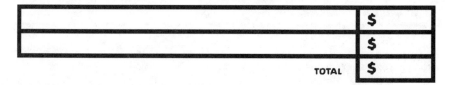

|  | $ |
|---|---|
|  | $ |
| TOTAL | $ |

HOW MANY HOURS DO YOU NEED TO WORK (INITIAL EXPENSE ÷ WAGE = TOTAL HOURS) IN ORDER TO PAY OFF YOUR INITIAL EXPENSES?

FINALLY, YOU NEED TO GET THE WORD OUT! WHAT ARE SOME WAYS THAT YOU CAN LET THE PEOPLE IN YOUR COMMUNITY KNOW THAT YOUR SERVICE IS AVAILABLE? MAKE A PLAN AND SET DEADLINES FOR YOURSELF IN ORDER TO GET STARTED. ASK FRIENDS AND FAMILY TO HELP YOU PUT OUT FLIERS AND SPREAD THE WORD!

## № 4 GETTING THE WORD OUT:

## № 5 DEADLINE:

# ENTREPRENEUR'S WORKSHEET:
# RAISING PIGS FOR PROFIT

## №1 INITIAL EXPENSES:

| | |
|---|---|
| HOUSING & FENCING SUPPLIES (HOG PANELS, ELECTRICAL FENCING, ETC.) | $ |
| FOOD & WATER SUPPLIES (TROUGH, WATERER, ETC.) | $ |
| PIG(S) | $ |

TOTAL $

IF YOU PLAN TO MAKE MONEY FROM SELLING YOUR PIGLETS AND/OR YOUR HOGS, THE INITIAL EXPENSES PAID TO RAISE YOUR PIG(S) ARE CONSIDERED AN INVESTMENT.

## №2 RECURRING EXPENSES:

| | |
|---|---|
| FOOD & WATER (VEGETABLES, PIG PELLETS, ALFALFA, ETC.) | $ |
| MEDICAL (ANNUAL WELLNESS CHECKS, MULTIVITAMINS, ETC.) | $ |
| MISC. (HOUSING/FENCING REPAIR, UNFORESEEN VET VISIT, ETC.) | $ |

TOTAL $

YOU MUST CONSIDER A FEW THINGS BEFORE YOU BEGIN: WHO WILL YOU MARKET TO? WILL YOU RAISE HOGS AND SELL THE PIGLETS AS FEEDER PIGS, OR RAISE PIGS TO MARKET WEIGHT? WILL YOU SELL THE WHOLE PIG OF MEAT CUTS? WHAT WILL YOUR COSTS BE WHILE THE PIGLETS GROW?

## №3

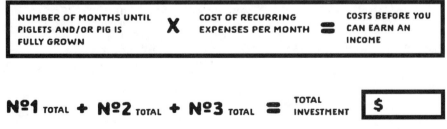

| NUMBER OF MONTHS UNTIL PIGLETS AND/OR PIG IS FULLY GROWN | **X** | COST OF RECURRING EXPENSES PER MONTH | **=** | COSTS BEFORE YOU CAN EARN AN INCOME |
|---|---|---|---|---|

**№1** TOTAL **+ №2** TOTAL **+ №3** TOTAL **=** TOTAL INVESTMENT $

# Acknowledgments

*The Hands-On Ranch Book* could not have come together without the efforts of our talented and hardworking staff at Five Marys.

Rebecca Lorenz, thank you for signing up to move to Fort Jones, California, to be a homeschool teacher for the girls on the ranch and for gracefully switching gears to teach all things ranch life to so many more eager learners all over the world through our M5 Ranch School! I appreciate your talents in writing, illustration, and editing, and I'm grateful for the many hours you dedicated to the curriculum of M5 Ranch School and the ideas in this book.

Riley Munn, thank you for your creative efforts that first found their outlet in the launch of M5 Ranch School—from designing the logo to creating illustrations for each and every lesson, many of which are included in *The Hands-On Ranch Book*.

Maddie Sorum, thank you for the hours you dedicated to developing the concept and curriculum of M5 Ranch School, all of which shaped the content of this book.

Katie Turner, thank you for sharing your knowledge and passion of horse husbandry and ranch life.

To our amazing M5 Community, thank you for sharing your talents, skills, expertise, and passion in various fields—from ice fishing to maple syrup making to natural herbs and wellness . . . and so many more interesting things.

Thank you to my faithful agent, Leslie Stoker, for your guidance and support on this book and all of the Five Marys endeavors!

And a big thank you to my editor, Andrea Doering, for believing in *The Hands-On Ranch Book*!

## MARY HEFFERNAN

and her husband, Brian, left behind the busy life they'd built in Silicon Valley to become cattle ranchers with their four young daughters—all named Mary. Together they own and operate Five Marys Farms, an 1,800-acre ranch in the mountains of Northern California where they live, work, and raise all-natural beef, pork, and lamb. Mary and Brian sell and ship directly from the farm to families all over the US. Five Marys was awarded Best Farm in America by *Paleo* magazine and has been featured in *Oprah* magazine, *Real Simple*, *Sunset*, and other national publications.